The First Time I Met Frank O'Hara

The First Time I Met Frank O'Hara

READING GAY AMERICAN WRITERS

by Rick Whitaker

PHOTOGRAPHS BY IANNIS DELATOLAS

FOUR WALLS EIGHT WINDOWS

NEW YORK/LONDON

Published in the United States by
Four Walls Eight Windows
39 West 14th Street
New York, NY 10011
http://www.4w8w.com

First printing September 2003

Cataloging-in-Publication Data for this book has been filed with the Library of Congress.

ISBN: 1-56858-272-2

Printed in the United States

10   9   8   7   6   5   4   3   2   1

For Jenny McPhee

I remember the first time I met Frank O'Hara. He was walking down Second Avenue. It was a cool early Spring evening but he was wearing only a white shirt with the sleeves rolled up to his elbows. And blue jeans. And moccasins. I remember that he seemed very sissy to me. Very theatrical. Decadent. I remember that I liked him instantly.

—Joe Brainard, *I Remember*

QUENTIN CRISP, "stately homo of England" and author of *The Naked Civil Servant, How to Become a Virgin, How to Have a Lifestyle,* and *Manners from Heaven,* notoriously said he would recommend aborting gay fetuses if they could be "diagnosed" early enough, suggesting that life as a homosexual in our reprobate world was too difficult and painful to justify. Certainly it has been and in some places (and in some families) still is a major hardship—even tragic—to be gay. But what's most impressive to me about the manner with which the best gay writers in the history of American literature have dealt with the difficulty of being sexually different from most of their peers is that far from complaining about it, or taking advantage of it and suing, even implicitly, for the reader's sympathy, each of them seems instead to have forged a new, unforeseen, unpredictable style. The homosexuality of each of the writers I have in mind, and the trouble such an illicit sexuality was capable of getting them into, made an important impact upon the ways they devised to compose poetry and prose—both what they chose to write about and how they wrote about it.

There is some quality—some element in the realm of the aesthetic—that is shared by most gay artists. Not *all* gay writers have it (Langston Hughes didn't have it, for instance, nor did Paul Bowles); and there are some straight writers who, it could be claimed, do have it (Elizabeth Hardwick, Thomas Bernhard). I cannot define it precisely, much less explain it. But this book is meant as an attempt to find out what *it* is. Each of the writers here demonstrates, in his or her work, what I will go ahead and call a gay sensibility. But the sensibility is expressed—the literary work is made—in a way that is completely different in each case, which is part of the meaning of the term: a gay sensibility is, above all, original and fresh. It also tends to be clever, scornful of laws, introspective, energetic, and sexy. There is often, in a gay sensibility, a degree of irony, and wit; and there is almost always a background of melancholy.

This book is not an academic study or a thorough survey of gay American literature, nor is it intended to be a definitive statement about the lives of gay writers, the nature of gay writing, or even gay literary history. It is just the written record of one writer's wrestling with a few of his betters, for the sport of it, and with the hope of thinking somewhat profitably about the meaning, and a few of the techniques, of becoming and being oneself. I am not an expert on anything at all, though I do have a passion for interesting sentences and poems, and I'm also moved by the cultural repercussions and the fruits, so to speak, of homosexuality. Though I have tried to make the book informative, it is not designed to instruct, though perhaps to persuade, if only of what may be already accepted as self-evidently true—that brooding, if only briefly, on these writers, and especially on their work, is rewarding in subtle and surprising ways.

I've written here only about writers and books I like or love; but I have not, of course, been able to write about *all* the gay American writers I admire. Some of them—Henry James, for example—would require time and space that I'm not able or competent to give. There seems little point in struggling to say something about a writer for the sake of having included him or her in my book. Joan Acocella's 2000 book on Willa Cather is a dazzling and sufficient enough commentary on that major gay writer for the time being, from my perspective. And what is there to say about a writer like Truman Capote? He wrote a perfect short novel (*Breakfast at Tiffany's*) and some other wonderful books, but criticism of Capote seems somehow beside the point. What one wants, aside from reading his books, is good gossip and anecdote about him, and there are already plenty of sources for that, including George Plimpton's book about him and a terrific book of conversations between Capote and Lawrence Grobel. About some important writers—Djuna Barnes, Elizabeth Bishop, James Merrill, Tennessee Williams—I have simply tried and failed to find something interesting and reasonably new to say. I've not even attempted to write about most of our younger gay writers, though I admire so many of them.

Nor have I chosen in every case to write about an author's most esteemed work. Whitman's poetry, for example, is probably considered to be of more lasting literary value than the letters he wrote after witnessing the deaths of soldiers during the Civil War. Likewise, Gore Vidal's best novel is not *The City and the Pillar*, but *Myra Breckinridge*. But there are dozens of books and thousands of essays about Whitman's poems, and besides, the letters actually affect *me* as much if not more than the poetry does; and in the case of Vidal, it seemed more interesting in the context of this book to compare his recent memoir to his early gay novel than merely to sing his praises, as so many have already done.

The only real "thread" that I have found running through the work of writers as unlike each other as Henry David Thoreau, Gertrude Stein, Hart Crane, and Jane Bowles is that each of them, to some extent, suffered the vicissitudes of difference, and each of them also *gained*, as a writer, from the experience of being more or less homosexual during periods of history when it was far more difficult than it is for most gay or bisexual people to be themselves now. As a result of being both inclined toward homosexuality and being unusually gifted, and thereby alienated again to some degree from the people around them, these writers were doubly bound (or enabled) to produce sentences, poems, novels that would be expressive of a complexity of feeling, or a special kind of feeling, that is probably accessible only to the sexual outsider. Their writing had to do for them what could not be accomplished by other means—to describe without describing, to show while hiding, to sing while keeping silent. What I love most in the best gay writing, in general, are the exciting moments in which I catch a glimpse of the author's true, sexual self—the part of himself or herself most anxiously and carefully protected and, perhaps for that reason, most deeply felt.

No one can really know now what it was like to be "gay" in the nineteenth century—it's among the lapses of history, since there is scarcely any record of homosexual practice, and precious little written reflection upon any homosexual experience, until well into the twentieth century (though due to the work of gay historians we are gradually learning what there is to know of our past). We do know that *something*, some persuasive force or internalized mandate, brought Walt Whitman—the most openly, musically enthusiastic celebrator of homosexual love in nineteenth-century America—to deny that he was gay when asked more or less directly. (He was not, of course, asked in those words: he was asked, by Englishman John Addington Symonds in a famous 1890 letter, if in his "conception of Comradeship," Whitman contemplated "the possible intrusion of those semi-sexual emotions and actions which no doubt do occur between men." Whitman's response was disappointing: that his poetry, or any selection from it, "has even allowed the possibility of such construction as mention'd is terrible.")

Thoreau may not have had sex with anyone, or was *very* discreet—
we'll probably never know the details of that famously recalcitrant
and reclusive genius's private life, though it is likely, judging from
his writings, that he was more gay than straight. Herman Melville
was apparently miserable most of his life, married and overburdened
and finally broken by the unhappiness that was the result of circumstances he seems to have grimly accepted rather than freely chosen.
Emily Dickinson, whose early letters to Susan Huntington attest to
her troubled and passionate love for the woman her brother later
married, spent the last twenty years of her life in her bedroom, alone,
sending down messages and flowers to visitors, her austere muse her
only intimate company.

‹◊›

I have lately found myself reading an inordinate number of gay writers. Even a few years ago, I would have thought of this as a little
embarrassing and strange, since I've been taught to look for and
appreciate great writing wherever it may be. Among my teachers
were Harold Bloom, Denis Donoghue, and Gordon Lish, of whom
none is gay. (Bloom did make a rather shocking confession to me
once, though. After asking me to promise him I would have only the
safest kind of sex, since he knew I was gay, he told me that he was
sorry not to have given "it" a try, and sorry he was "too old" to get
started at the time, in the early '90s.)

Why have I lately been so strongly drawn, in my reading, toward
my fellow queers? What is it about their work in particular that is so
engaging and important for me? What distinguishes the work of
these gay writers from that of most of their straight contemporaries?
I've sought not so much for definite answers to such questions as to

question my motives as a reader, and to explore the tendency within myself to drift toward these writers and their work. Ultimately, I know, it doesn't really matter *why* I have such a crush on the work of so many gay writers; what matters is the writing, and above all the element of surprise we find therein, which is what I believe we all love most about art in general.

Ralph Waldo Emerson, in an 1860 book called *The Conduct of Life,* wrote that "The only path of escape known in all the worlds of God is performance. You must do your work, before you shall be released." In the work of any great writer, from a reader's perspective, the most exciting and ultimately the most interesting aspect of the writing is extremely subtle—it is, finally, the writer's "way with words," his unique relation to syntax and signification. But another of the pleasures associated, for me, with immersion in a great writer's body of work, and particularly in the case of the gay Americans discussed here, is the growing sense, as I read, that the writer, in a variety of ways, is earning release: from the tyranny of imposed silence, from the oppression of the closet, from a sense of earthboundedness, from dailiness, from the sad human condition of life-and-death-and-then-nothing-at-all. The spiritual aspects of release may, of course, be merely symbolic. But like the concept of God, which may also correspond to an emptiness—a myth—the idea of release is not without meaning. If an aspiration for release is part of the spiritual motivation for artists, then perhaps it makes some sense to bear that aspiration in mind as we read. It is possible—I have no doubt—to achieve release if we do our work, even if the work we do is a performance only for the solitary audience that watches from within.

Reading is an intimate activity; the relation between reader and text is similar, in a way, to that between one person and another. The gradualness of discovery, the tendency not to reveal every secret straightaway, the unpredictability of what will come next, the beauty, the pleasure of engagement: books are not completely unlike people, nor is reading a book completely unlike getting to know someone.

I never met Frank O'Hara (he was killed by a dune buggy on the beach in 1966, two years before I was born); but I remember the first time I met his poetry. It was a cool early spring evening, I believe. I remember that I liked him instantly.

The Nineteenth Century

FITZ-GREENE HALLECK (1790–1867), who lived during both the War of 1812 and the Civil War, was brazenly homosexual well before there was such a word in the language or such a category for human beings. (The term *homosexual* was first used in Germany in 1868, but it took several decades for it to be commonly used.) Halleck was also among the most famous of American poets, if not *the* most famous, in the middle of the nineteenth century. In 1864 the *New York Times* endorsed him as the unofficial national poet, and Edgar Allen Poe wrote twenty years earlier that "No name in the American poetical world is more firmly established than that of Fitz-Greene Halleck." A statue of him on Central Park's "Literary Walk" is still today the only representation there of an American writer; it was unveiled in 1877 by President Hayes and a crowd of *fifty thousand people*. Halleck dined twice with President Jackson; Abraham Lincoln complimented him; and John Quincy Adams referred to his poetry in a speech to the House of Representatives in 1836. For sixteen years he was "a sort of secretary and companion" to John Jacob Astor, America's richest and best-connected man. Halleck was admired by Charles Dickens, William Thackeray, James Fenimore Cooper, Washington Irving, and especially Poe.

But by 1930, he was largely forgotten.

John W. M. Halleck, the poet's "distant relative" and the author of *The American Byron: Homosexuality and the Fall of Fitz-Greene Halleck* (2000), believes that Halleck's eventual exclusion from the pantheon of great poets, his "radical fall from fame,"

demonstrates "the politics of decanonization, just as his decanonization negates his significant contributions to American verse and sexual ideology." Halleck was apparently quite the flamboyant dandy.
The statue of him in Central Park is of an ultra-elegant gentleman
holding a fountain pen, with his pinky finger curved delicately in the
air and a soft, poetical thought on the tip of his dainty tongue. Hallock, the academic biographer, credits his subject with not only
being a great poet, but also—more accurately—with changing the

way the world, and Americans in particular, thought about love between people of the same sex in the nineteenth century. "Halleck's love for another man [i.e. Joseph Rodman Drake] contributed to the dismantling of the platonic framework of Romantic idealism." Halleck never pretended that his love for Drake, or his lust for other men, was anything other than sexual and consuming; it was not just friendship.

The day Drake died at the tender age of twenty-five on September 21, 1820, Halleck, who was desperately in love with him, wrote a poem—the first of several memorial lyrics he would compose about Drake—that would be published within a year in four major American periodicals, including the popular *New York Evening Post*. It was Poe's favorite among Halleck's poems. Reading it never fails to send a chill down my own spine. The poem's epigraph, by Wordsworth, sets the tone, restrained and formal but at the same time fiercely passionate and tormented:

> The good die first,
> And they, whose hearts are dry as summer dust,
> Burn to the socket.

The last short line of the epigraph refers strangely to an empty space, but it's unclear in this excerpt *whose* "hearts are dry as summer dust": the hearts of the dead, or of some other "they" who live on, dry and burning—the less good, who will die later.

Halleck then begins his poem, "On the Death of Joseph Rodman Drake, of New York, Sept. 1820," by looking sadly to the future, when his beloved will have been buried awhile. The first word of his poem, *green*, is creepy by contrast with its common associations, particularly in nineteenth-century poetry, to lush, summer country; green seems the wrong color altogether with which to begin a poem of mourning, and we're instantly aware of other incongruities—terrible, troubling ones.

> Green be the turf above thee,
>   Friend of my better days!
> None knew thee but to love thee,
>   Nor named thee but to praise.
>
> Tears fell when thou wert dying,
>   From eyes unused to weep,
> And long, where thou art lying,
>   Will tears the cold turf steep.
>
> When hearts, whose truth was proven,
>   Like thine, are laid in earth,
> There should a wreath be woven
>   To tell the world their worth;
>
> And I who woke each morrow
>   To clasp thy hand in mine,
> Who shared thy joy and sorrow,
>   Whose weal and woe were thine:
>
> It should be mine to braid it
>   Around thy faded brow,
> But I've in vain essayed it,
>   And feel I cannot now.

> While memory bids me weep thee,
> Nor thoughts nor words are free,
> The grief is fixed too deeply
> That mourns a man like thee.

This is a beautiful poem and an astonishing document in the history of gay American literature, one of the few great exceptions to the general rule during the nineteenth century of discretion and indirectness. While it's true that such a text was created within a literary tradition of relatively innocent male friendship (described by Caleb Crain in his 2001 *American Sympathy: Men, Friendship, and Literature in the New Nation*), I believe this poem, unusually, goes beyond that tradition—it steps just past the boundary of friendship, helplessly (and successfully) using Drake's tragic death as the justification for its outright homoeroticism.

Halleck gives in to an expression in this poem of uncontrollable feeling, confessing by implication that Drake was, in fact, his lover: the poet woke each morning to clasp Drake's hand, to share his feelings, whatever they might be. He wept while Drake was dying, and "long, where thou art lying, / Will tears the cold turf steep."

The poet then goes on to suggest that it should fall to him, and not, therefore, to Drake's widow, to make a wreath and braid it round the dead man's "faded brow." But he has tried "in vain" to show the depth and intensity of his feelings for Drake before, and "cannot now." He's paralyzed, in shock; he is at a loss.

‹◊›

When Halleck lived in Greenwich Village, in the early years of the nineteenth century, most Americans were probably fairly clueless about what two bachelors might want to get up to together in an all-male boarding house. Sodomy legislation at the time outlawed not only same-sex relations but also masturbation, fellatio, bestiality, and just about anything physically lewd that didn't lead intentionally (and within wedlock) to reproduction. Halleck, who was famous and visible in the city and in the highest circles of society, hid nothing from anyone. "He openly expressed physical disdain for women," Hallock writes; "his 'central emotional direction' was toward men, to whom he was intensely attracted." He was elected poet laureate of the Ugly Club, a group of New York's "handsomest men" that held all-male balls on Wall Street. Remarking upon his duty as best man in Drake's wedding, Halleck wrote to his sister and confidante, "He is, perhaps, the handsomest man in New York, . . . I felt myself during the ceremony as committing a crime in aiding and assisting in such a sacrifice."

Halleck moved from Guilford, Connecticut, to New York City in 1811 when he was twenty-one and still considered good-looking. He loved the city immediately: it was "a source of pleasure hitherto unknown" for him "to trace the endless variety of man, to mark the different propositions, passions, and pursuits" of his new acquaintances and neighbors—mostly working-class men in boarding houses like the one Halleck stayed in. He had an early crush on James B., one of his coworkers in a Quaker banking firm: "a fine young fellow," he wrote again to his sister, "very pretty-looking—I say pretty, for he has quite a boyish appearance." It was mutual lust, if not love, at first sight—at least it was mutual according to Halleck's interpretation of the young man's friendliness. "On my first entrance into the office, he appeared very anxious to form an intimacy with me; his condescending and amiable manners soon endeared him to *me*, and we vowed eternal friendship when we had hardly seen each other an hour." The affair with James B., however, did not last for long; like most of the men with whom Halleck became involved, James eventually married, a fate Halleck often lamented in his poetry. His last major poem, "Young America," is a long, cynical song about a teenage boy who faces his next birthday with the grim resolve to become mercenary even if he must be compromised. It opens happily enough, a vision of pastoral calm and youthful promise:

> It is a boy whom fourteen years have seen,
> Smiling, with them, on spring's returning green,
> A bonny boy, with eye-delighting eyes,
> Sparkling as stars, and blue as summer's skies,
> With face, like April's, bright in smiles or tears,
> His laugh a song—his step the forest deer's,
> With heart as pure and liberal as the air,
> And voice of sweetest tone, and bright gold hair
> In thick curls clustering round his even brow,
> And dimpled cheek—how calm he slumbers now!

But, having shifted to the first person, it ends in the opposite mood on the eve of the boy's fifteenth birthday:

> I've seen the world, and by the world been seen,
> And now am speeding fast upon the way
> To the calm, quiet evening of my day;
> There but remains one promise to fulfil,
> I bow myself obedient to its will,
> And am prepared to settle down in life
> By wooing—winning—wedding A RICH WIFE.

The First Time I Met Frank O'Hara

‹◊›

Halleck met the very handsome and sophisticated Joseph Drake in 1813, only to "lose" him a year later to marriage. But *this* intimate friendship would actually survive matrimony—the two men were very close until Drake's untimely death. Halleck assumed (probably with good reason) that his dashing friend's marriage to the rich, unattractive Sarah Eckford was simply a matter of social and economic upward movement—Halleck was annoyed and disappointed by their marriage, but not heartbroken. To distract himself, he took several trips, always preferring to travel alone, but found Philadelphia, Baltimore, and Washington, D.C. far inferior to New York, though he was thrilled to catch a glimpse of the glamorous Dolley Madison at a theater in the capital city. Most of the time, Halleck and Drake were inseparable in Manhattan, particularly from 1817 until Drake's death three years later. Their relationship was taken as a romantic model for Bayard Taylor's 1870 genteel novel *Joseph and His Friend*, and Halleck and Drake also turn up as minor characters in Gore Vidal's 1973 historical novel *Burr*.

In their glory days together, Halleck and Drake anonymously published a series of poems, many of which they wrote in collaboration with each other. These poems, known as "The Croakers," were lighthearted and often funny. "To Mrs. Barnes, the actress" was among their joint efforts, and it strikes now the definite chord of a rollicking gay sensibility.

> Away with passion's withering kiss,
>   A purer spell be thine to win us;
> Unlock the fount of holiness

While gentle Pity weeps in bliss,
And hearts throb sweetly sad within us.

These are the overwrought thoughts of ironic aesthetes, who long for high camp disguised as the exhibition of pure feeling—a few of whom still exist all over the world, now known simply as one among many varieties of gay men. Was Drake gay? Nobody knows. Was Halleck? Certainly, though it is a matter only for speculation just how aware he was that he was not only *unlike* the majority of men, but *like* many others. In a society in which the official punishment for sodomy was death, Halleck was amazingly open about his feelings for Drake and his desire for the intimate company of men. But neither he nor Drake could have had any idea that their blithe poems were the first published expressions in the United States of what would become a long tradition leading eventually to what we think of as a literary gay culture. It's uncanny that Drake, who married and was unable or unwilling to devote himself exclusively to Halleck and died young, should have been a collaborator in the creation of a culture that embraced difference, confusion, irony, and youth along with passion, excellence, and the struggle for the perfection of artistic talent.

It was Drake himself, not Halleck, who wrote perhaps the gayest of all the "Croakers," a poem that looks forward to Oscar Wilde and the wish for pleasure as opposed to happiness, the *effect* rather than the real, the ability to turn plain life into fabulous art or at least sophisticated fun.

The man who frets at worldly strife,
Grows sallow, sour, and thin;
Give us the lad whose happy life
Is one perpetual grin;

The First Time I Met Frank O'Hara

He, Midas-like, turns all to gold,
He smiles when others sigh,
Even alike the hot and cold,
And laughs through wet and dry.

WHILE HALLECK pursued his very public life in New York City as poet, man-about-town, and secretary to Astor, a completely different sort of proto-gay man in Concord, Massachusetts, came to fit the description in Drake's Croaker of an adult who "grows sallow, sour, and thin." Henry David Thoreau's life and work initiated an American tradition in sharp contrast with that of the campy, emotional style of Drake and Halleck. I'm among the countless readers of Thoreau's *Walden, or, Life in the Woods* who have found in Thoreau (1817–1892) a complex model, reliable inspiration, and above all a partner in the conversation we all have about how we should live—a conversation that never stops, at least not for long.

After a year and a half of living in the country, I've decided (as I write this) to move back to the city in the fall. I'll be leaving upstate New York, I like to think, for "as good a reason as I went there," as Thoreau says of his departure from the woods in the grand "Conclusion" to *Walden*. He explains his decision to leave his handmade hut at age thirty—two years younger than I am now—and go back to a more populated existence, back to the small town of Concord, two miles away, where he lived in the attic of his parents' house, back to "civilized life" and a way of living that would appear more ordinary: "Perhaps it seemed to me that I had several more lives to live, and could not spare any more time for that one. It is remarkable how easily and insensibly we fall into a particular route, and make a beaten track for ourselves." Like the basis for almost all of Thoreau's tropes, his "beaten track" was real—it was a dirt path he'd "insensibly" made between his cabin and the pond. "The surface of the earth is soft and impressible... and so with the paths which the mind travels." The mind, like the body, tends to beat down particular routes to predictable places, and for Thoreau, to live repetitively, aware of nothing more exalted than "our dullest perception" and common sense, is barely to live at all. "The commonest sense is the sense of men asleep, which they express by snoring."

I started to read *Walden* because it was a book I'd always meant to read, and it seemed like a good idea to read it while I was living in the country. I hoped it would help me to appreciate all of the natural things I'm surrounded by here—trees and bugs and weather. And it did. Though I know comparatively little about plants and animals, reading *Walden* has deepened my awareness of the godlike quality in natural things, and confirmed my timid belief in a friendly, protective power with which I can feel myself to be in mysterious communication. But the surprising effect of reading *Walden* has been the firming-up of my decision to get back to the more secular, more "civilized" life of the city. The country has its exotic horizons and its striking, disconcerting distances between large-scale objects, but I know now that "it is easier to sail many thousand miles through cold and storm and cannibals... than it is to explore the private sea, the Atlantic and Pacific Ocean of one's being alone." And though I have been lonely at times in the country, my "private sea" is really in the city, where my being alone means something to me and isn't just a hard natural fact.

Thoreau denies that he was ever lonely while he lived alone at Walden Pond. The winter storms were all "merry," the evenings all "cheerful," the open fire (before he brought in a stove the second winter he was there) the only company he required. Yet near the end of *Walden*, he writes one of the loneliest little paragraphs in American literature.

There too, as everywhere, I sometimes expected the Visitor who never comes. The Vishnu Purana says, "The householder is to remain at eventide in his courtyard as long as it takes to milk a cow, or longer if he pleases, to await the arrival of a guest." I often performed this duty of hospitality, waited long enough to milk a whole herd of cows, but did not see the man approaching from the town.

Thoreau was not a good-looking man. Nathaniel Hawthorne said he was "as ugly as sin, long-nosed, queer-mouthed, and with uncouth and somewhat rustic, although courteous manners." A Concord woman who knew Thoreau described him as "a thin, insignificant, poorly dressed, careless looking young man." In 1843, he lived for six months on Staten Island, of all places, but then moved back to Concord because life on Staten Island was too hectic and complicated, and he was soon homesick and adrift. He went to school at Harvard, but spent most of his short life (he died at forty-four) in and around Concord. He famously went to jail for one night, and he lived for a while with the Emersons, but mostly he lived alone in his attic bedroom. He proposed marriage to Ellen Sewall by letter, and was rejected—she seemed unable to take him seriously as a lover.

Thoreau also wrote a tender, erotic poem to Miss Sewall's eleven-year-old brother, Edmund. The poem, "Sympathy," concerns the narrator's regret that the boy, inevitably, was growing up, moving gloriously into the world, but irretrievably away from the intimate friendship with Thoreau that was apparently among the writer's most sentimentally engaging, romantic experiences as a young man. The first stanza:

> Lately, alas, I knew a gentle boy,
>> Whose features all were cast in Virtue's mould,
> As one she had designed for Beauty's toy,
>> But after manned him for her own stronghold.

There are hints (such as that *alas* in the first line) that Thoreau was gay at many places in his writings, particularly in his journals. For example, when he was twenty-three he wrote appreciatively: "These young buds of manhood in the streets are like buttercups in the meadows. . . ." And later the thirty-five-year-old bachelor wrote, after complaining of how tedious he found an evening party made up of "mostly young women, in a small room, warm and noisy": "The society of young women is the most unprofitable I have ever tried. They are so light and flighty that you can never be sure whether they are there or not there. I prefer to talk with the more staid and settled, *settled for life*, in every sense." While living at Walden, he wrote, "What the difference is between man and woman—that they should be so attracted to one another I never saw adequately stated." And he continues in the same entry: "I love men with the same distinction that I love woman—as if my friend were of some third sex," using, as Michael Warner points out in his brilliant 1992 article, "Thoreau's Bottom," a curious inconsistency between "men" in the plural (as if he had real men in mind) and "woman" as an abstract category.

At Walden, he claimed, he could "always see a face in the fire" and therefore had no need for the society of people. He was glad to be alone. After all, "God is alone,—but the devil, he is far from being alone; he sees a great deal of company; he is legion."

Thoreau refused to be lonely—it was an important aspect of his aesthetic philosophy and his life as a writer. He was emphatic: "I am no more lonely than the Mill Brook, or a weathercock, or the north star, or the south wind, or an April shower, or a January thaw, or the first spider in a new house." But his loneliness at the pond has always been apparent to his readers and biographers, and it clearly never got much better for him after he moved back to Concord. In 1857, ten years after he left Walden, he wrote in his journal (which was published in fourteen lengthy volumes), "...cold and solitude are friends of mine.... I come to my solitary woodland walk as the home-sick go home."

<〈◇〉>

Long before he moved out to the pond, Thoreau was very close to Emerson, who was becoming famous as a writer and the founder of American Transcendentalism, a quasi-philosophical movement that aimed to reconcile ideas originating in the work of Kant, Locke, and Hume with religious concepts from Calvinism and the Quakers, along with Emerson's own ideas, particularly about the priority of individualism. Three years before Thoreau took full-time to the woods, Emerson published an article in which he quoted from William Sewel's *History of the Quakers*: "Go not to men for a creed, faint not, but be of good courage. The darkness is only for a season. We must be willing to tarry the Lord's time in the wilderness, if we would enter the Promised Land. The purest saints that I have ever known were long, very long, in darkness and in doubt. Even when they had firm faith, they were long without *feeling* what they *believed in*. One told me he was two years in chaotic darkness, without an inch of firm ground to stand upon, watching for the dayspring from on high...." Thoreau spent two years, two months, and two days more or less alone in the woods. He was Emerson's pre-eminent student, and his decision to live apart from other people had Emerson's approval: it was on Emerson's land that he built his hut. His retreat was as much a public, open experiment in Transcendentalism as it was a private act of intellectual good faith. Among his missions in going to live alone at the pond was surely proving to himself, to Emerson, and to whomever else would pay attention, that an individual could thrive on nothing but the bare necessities and a true effort to know God, which for Thoreau at that time was the same as getting to know nature. As for finding some "firm ground" upon which to stand, Thoreau even attempted to find the bottom of Walden Pond, which the people of Concord had always assumed to be bottomless. Thoreau sounded the bottom with a cod line and a stone. He was glad to find that the pond was deep. "What if all ponds were shallow? Would it not react on the minds of men? I am thankful that this pond was made deep and pure for a symbol. While men believe in the infinite, some ponds will be thought to be bottomless."

Most of *Walden* is made of sentences that describe simple, natural phenomena that are meant to transcend their sensuality and to take on, in the context of the writing, the complexity of advanced human thought. "I awoke to an answered question, to Nature and daylight," Thoreau writes in the section of *Walden* called "The Pond in Winter." He'd been troubled with a vague question throughout the night—or an interrogative feeling. When he woke up and saw "dawning Nature, in whom all creatures live," he realized that Nature had "no question on *her* lips," and so he, a natural person as each of us is at heart, could consider his question answered, or rather not bother to ask it. In this way, Thoreau consoles himself repeatedly by stating his faith that we needn't look for the answers because we don't even know the important questions. His strategy is to accept the world and his situation in it, and to train himself (and us, his readers) to appreciate, and not merely survive, these conditions. What he doesn't quite know what to do with, though, is his anxiety and loneliness.

And now I find myself in a similar quandary. The point, for me, of living in the country has been to have an intense experience of my feelings and thoughts—to nurture calm, so that my real self can speak and be heard. Being around lots of people all the time, as I was in the city, I'm inevitably influenced by them, and I feel that I should rather influence myself now, or at least narrow the influences down, so that I can *have* my own thoughts. And I want to *feel* my thoughts. "How shall I help myself?" Thoreau asks. "By withdrawing into the garret, and associating with spiders and mice, determining to meet myself face to face sooner or later. Completely silent and attentive I will be this hour, and the next, and forever." But for Thoreau and for me, the world intrudes and seduces—because the world is actually another word for life, and the lonely garret is full of anxiety.

‹◊›

"My purpose in going to Walden Pond was . . . to transact some private business. . . ." Thoreau in 1845, when he moved into his cabin on Independence Day, was a twenty-eight-year-old intellectual. He'd done some work in the family pencil-making factory and had made some real improvements in the quality of the pencils. He had also taught children both in schools and as a private tutor. But he didn't feel especially suited for either kind of work, and he was never employed in one place for long. "All men want . . . something to *do*, or rather something to *be*." The month Thoreau left Walden, September, 1847, he answered a letter concerning the tenth anniversary of his graduation from Harvard. Among the routine questions was what sort of work the graduate was now doing—what he *was*. He answered that he was many things—a farmer, a house painter, a carpenter, a mason, a day laborer, a pencil maker, a writer. But "my steadiest employment, if such it can be called," he wrote, "is to keep myself at the top of my condition, and ready for whatever may turn up in heaven or on earth." He helped build a house, also on Walden Pond, for the Emersons. Bronson Alcott, a friend, designed the house so poorly, and it was so ugly, that it was never lived in. Everyone but Alcott knew it was a travesty from the very beginning, but it had "turned up" and Thoreau was ready. That was what he did, or what he *was*.

What am I? A writer, yes, and lately a counselor in a home for developmentally disabled children, a homosexual, a dog owner, a house renter. But here in the country I am a tourist, a visitor, an unmethodical observer from the city. "At last, we know not what it is to live in the open air, and our lives are domestic in more senses than we think. From the hearth to the field is a great distance." Thoreau was right. Yesterday I took Louise, the dog, to a pond I know up on a hill, surrounded by woods. I let her off the leash to play on the ice, and she immediately ran into the woods and disappeared. I tromped through the snow in pursuit and having become completely lost I came out onto a large field. I listened hard for Louise, and heard—nothing. I wanted to find my dog and take her home. I found my way back to the pond, and I was ecstatic when (hours later) Louise came running, and we jumped in the car and drove toward town. When it comes to being essentially domestic—even "in more senses than we think"—I stand guilty as charged. I confess that I prefer a familiar backyard, or parts of Central Park, to an eerie open field.

In the chapter on "Solitude," Thoreau recalls: "Some of my pleasantest hours were during the long rainstorms in the spring or fall, which confined me to the house for the afternoon as well as the forenoon, soothed by their ceaseless roar and pelting; when an early twilight ushered in a long evening in which many thoughts had time to take root and unfold themselves." Such a scene fills me with a mix of longing and dread. The "ceaseless roar and pelting" along with "an early twilight" remind me of dreary days as a child, when Dad seemed to come home earlier than usual, and bedtime loomed all evening, and I was miserable watching *Hawaii Five-O* on TV. My feelings on rainy days now are less predictable. There's a part of me that, as a reader of *Walden*, longs to be like Thoreau says he was, soothed by the rain, thoughtful and patient; and I also want to believe Thoreau is telling the truth and holding nothing back. But I sense a darker reality behind his happy words. I feel sure that Thoreau did have many fine days and evenings on his own at the pond, and enjoyed his solitude and had some peace of mind, and loved being close to the woods and the animals and his God. But if he was so happy alone in his cabin, why did he leave? He says he had "more lives" to live—but why wasn't that one life enough? I wish he'd been able to overcome the mental ruts and the habits and the dull routine without needing to shuffle back to Concord. "We are the subjects of an experiment," he says. And "I find it wholesome to be alone the greater part of the time." But why, then, couldn't he stay put and live out the interesting experiment? And why, I ask myself, does it matter so much to me?

I'm always on the verge of a new theory about my life and always looking for material—in poetry and prose, in art and in the lives of other people and other species—to back up my fledgling axioms. I'm led to particular books by a wonderful divination that is more reliable to me than any logic or education. And Thoreau, it seems, wrote *Walden* precisely in order to help himself and other people to find a way of living that is worthy of us, given our privileged physical freedom and our intimacy with the enormous world arrayed so beautifully before us—we can see the land, and taste its fruits, and hear the way it rattles and sings. We can take bits of the natural world into our hands and love them—we can describe the plants and the animals, observe the seasons, plant crops and cut wood and walk a mile and swim in a pond. With all these blessings (and the attendant anxiety), we require a system of expression—and a form of life—that isn't reducible to a trivial accumulation of days and nights. We must find out how to live—and where to live, and what to *be*.

In the chapter "Where I Lived, and What I Lived For," Thoreau writes about his preparations for settling in at Walden. He spent an afternoon, which he says was all it took, deciding just where his little house should go, which trees he wanted to see from his window. And then he did nothing else toward arranging things around his presence there, "for a man is rich in proportion to the number of things which he can afford to let alone." Reading *Walden* has helped me to free myself from certain encumbrances. I'm learning to let things alone—things like the cultural experience of my friends, and some of the detritus of old bad habits such as gambling and taking drugs for fun, and my own conception of God, which is really just a combination of nature and psychology, but bigger than the sum of those parts. I'm beginning to learn that things will not only continue to exist without my meddling—they may even prosper and grow. When Thoreau commands his reader to live "as long as possible . . . free and uncommitted," in the past I might have willfully understood him to be approving of recklessness and promiscuity. Now I read it as a warn-

ing against being too materialistic and busy. The point for me now is to be devoted to something worthwhile, for example the development of myself both as a citizen of the world and as an independent spiritual entity. Uncommitted, but not unengaged. "Moral reform is the effort to throw off sleep," Thoreau says. My tendency to sleep, in the moral sense, is perhaps the one thing I can't afford to let alone.

Thoreau's philosophical and spiritual practice is perhaps best described, in the chapter on "Sounds," as "the discipline of looking always at what is to be seen." To sustain contact with a godlike entity requires vigilance, though not necessarily work. "There were times when I could not afford to sacrifice the bloom of the present moment to any work, whether of the head or hands." He spent long summer mornings at Walden doing nothing that an outsider could have judged (though they—his neighbors—did judge him for doing nothing); he sat in his "sunny doorway from sunrise till noon, rapt in a reverie." Such were his most productive hours of all. "I grew in those seasons like corn in the night. . . ." For me, sitting still and doing nothing is a challenge, and not one I can face every day, even for a few minutes. I want to read, or listen to music, or clean the house. I have been cultivating stillness, but so far it has only sprouted. I anticipate the full blossom of serenity, and I will continue to do what I can toward that end—I will keep looking at what is to be seen. And it's good to know that wherever I am, among people or trees, in the quiet daylight or the flash of the streets, the "experiment" will always continue so long as I keep myself experimental.

‹◊›

Thoreau was increasingly interested in the scientific ordering and understanding of nature as he neared the end of his short life. He shifted the emphasis of his studious devotion from Emerson the poet-philosopher to Darwin the naturalist-theorist. His curiosity led him away from himself toward the macrocosmic. But Thoreau never forgot that mathematical precision is a matter of indifference to the natural world—it is people who perform the experiments, and it is only people who admire them. There is no question on nature's lips. It's not so much natural events or classifications that matter for us, but how they can be a meaningful part of our lives. "The fact which interests us most is the life of the naturalist," Thoreau says in his first book, *A Week on the Concord and Merrimack Rivers*. "The purest science is still biographical." The *life* of the naturalist, not the naturalism.

Toward the end of his life Thoreau was compiling a sort of nature journal, recently published as *Wild Fruits*, in which he recorded as much of what he saw happening outdoors as he could put down on paper, in words. Much of the writing is extremely spare and factual; some of it simply takes note of Thoreau's observations. One complete entry, for example, concerns wool-grass, whatever that is: "Wool-grass with its brown heads, August nineteenth." There is a kind of poetry to such an austere practice, but I myself don't fully understand the obsession he had with plants and with making such endless notes about them. Yet I admire his passionate resolve to sustain the effort regardless of the world's apparent indifference, which he must have felt—the manuscript has just been published for the first time more than 135 years after his death. He must have believed that he was doing God's work, in some sense or another. And this very strange, uninviting last book of his is also a reminder, as he says in the preface, that "it is the spirit in which you do a thing which makes it interesting, whether it is sweeping a room or pulling turnips."

I remember hearing once that John Cage (who loved Thoreau's work) was asked what one should do if bored by something. Keep doing it, Cage replied, and eventually it won't be boring anymore. Alone in a cabin by a lovely pond, pulling turnips and watching the wool-grass grow, I think I'd go nuts before long. But I do have just enough faith to believe that if I did it for long enough, in a spirit of freedom and cheerfulness, it would become interesting to me. I'm just not sure that doing other things—elsewhere—wouldn't be *more* interesting.

The city beckons as I sit here in my placid country room, the dog asleep, a single fly making all the noise I can hear apart from the hum of my computer and the ticking of the clock. "Often, in the repose of my midday," Thoreau wrote, "there reaches my ears a confused *tintinnabulum* from without. It is the noise of my contemporaries." What is the noise of *my* contemporaries? What's happening in the city? What am I going back to? I want to overcome the need to be consoled; I want to accept things as they are—but how are they? We will never really know, the Age of Information notwithstanding. Even the most avid collector of news, the most observant traveler, the most adept web surfer, gets only tiny fragments of the world—random reports by interested parties, with an advertising banner across the top. We can only hope that we, like Thoreau, can awake one day to find "dawning Nature, in whom all creatures live, looking in at [our] broad windows with serene and satisfied face. . . ." In the way saints used to imitate Christ, we can aspire to imitate "the natural day," which "is very calm."

I still find myself wondering what to do with myself most days as I more or less blindly go about my chores and pleasures. I feel as if I never make much progress along a path that goes someplace magnificent; but I just continue on past changing scenery in the company of my own cast of characters, some of whom I love. "I went to the woods because I wished to live deliberately, to front only the essential facts of life, and see if I could not learn what it had to teach, and not, when I came to die, discover that I had not lived." I don't worry much about finding that I hadn't lived—I have lived, and I'm living now. That much I have come to know. But I would like to have a reliable idea, or to be more confident in my instincts, when it comes to living in a way that I can feel good about in the long run. I'm not happy thinking only of myself, and I'm not honestly concerned about helping everyone. "To affect the quality of the day, that is the highest of the arts," Thoreau says. And so if living is itself an art, then I can live to affect the quality of the day, and I can rest assured that that will be work I can do wherever I am.

A voice came to John Farmer, Thoreau's country neighbor, in the chapter from *Walden* on "Higher Laws," to ask Farmer why he stayed to "live this mean moiling life, when a glorious existence is possible" elsewhere. "All that he could think of," Thoreau writes, "was to practice some new austerity, to let his mind descend into his body and redeem it, and treat himself with ever-increasing respect." Which sounds like a fable— the one we've all heard at some point in our lives about the man or woman who discovers himself or herself to be nothing more or less than a natural creature whose "whole life is startlingly moral" and who is somehow never alone.

I'M SPENDING THE SUMMER—still in the country—in an old, restored farmhouse that belongs to a friend who was away for a while but has now come home. He bought the house (situated forty miles from the nearest cinema and four hours from New York City) with his long-time companion, who died several years ago; now my friend lives in the house year-round by himself. Understandably, he likes to talk when there's someone to talk to, and most of his stories concern his career as a dancer and choreographer in New York, Israel, and on tour. Sometimes, though, he talks about his childhood and his family. He was born into a large Italian immigrant family in Chicago in the 1930s. He has three sisters and a brother. A few years ago, his mother died. (His father had died years before.) My friend, who had been invited every year for decades to a family holiday party held on New Year's Day in Chicago, decided the time had come for him to go to the party and spend some time with his siblings, who were all older than he (who was then in his late sixties). He telephoned one of his sisters and told her he was coming to Chicago for the holidays and would stay for twelve days. Why so long? his sister asked him. Where will you stay? You'd better call so-and-so, another of his sisters. And so it went with all three of the sisters and his brother: they all wondered why he should want to stay in Chicago for as long as twelve days, and they all wondered where he would stay (his plan had been to spend a few nights with each of them). They all had children and grandchildren, cousins, and other various relatives coming, and not one of them invited my friend to spend even a night in their home. Finally my friend told them to just forget about it, that he wouldn't come after all, that it had been a terrible mistake to consider it. But having already paid for a plane ticket to Chicago, he phoned a friend in the city, a woman writer who had cancer and wasn't expected to live more than a year longer (and who is now dead) and described to her the reaction of his family to his plan of coming to Chicago for the party. She immediately invited him to spend the entire twelve days with her, sleeping on her convertible sofa in the living room, and he accepted her offer. A young nephew in Chicago—who happens to be gay, like my friend—drove him to and from the family's New Year's Day party, where he enjoyed the same cool, unsatisfying relations with his siblings that he had for the last fifty or so years. The point of my friend's story, he told me, was that all the talk of big happy close Italian families was "total bullshit." Depend on your friends, he advised me—not on your family.

Walt Whitman (1819-1892) also came from a large family. He was born in Brooklyn and had a sister and five brothers, of whom one was crippled and retarded, one suffered from tertiary syphilis, and one was an alcoholic with tuberculosis. One of his brothers, though, George, had a brilliant career as a soldier in the Civil War—he was promoted eventually to major. Slightly wounded in Fredericksburg, Virginia (a shell exploded at his feet, and a bit of shrapnel entered his cheek), George was listed in the December 16, 1862, *New York Tribune* as among the casualties of the Fifty-first New York Regiment. Alarmed and worried, Walt left Brooklyn within an hour of getting the news, determined to find his brother, dead or alive, in Virginia. When, at long last, he found him in good health and good spirits, he wrote to their mother right away, and mentioned how completely his own considerable problems and difficulties (including being robbed on the train) had "vanished into nothing."

But in George's prolific wartime journal and his subsequent letters home, there is never a word about Walt: neither of his arrival, his activities, nor his departure. "A man's family," Whitman wrote many years later, "is the people who love him—the people who comprehend him."

Whitman, like many of the gay men that came after him, eventually found a "family" among the people who loved him and comprehended him—including the fans of his poetry (many of whom were gay men), his friends, and the wounded and dying men he encountered first in New York hospitals and later during the Civil War.

‹◊›

Whitman began visiting hospitalized young men in New York City in the 1850s, long before the war. Most of these sick or injured men were stagecoach drivers Whitman had met while riding up and down Broadway with them. Stagecoach driving was a hazardous occupation—the men were mostly hurt from having been run over by their own wagons, beaten by roving gangs such as the Plug Uglies or the Roach Guards, or from fights with other drivers. Some of them were dangerously ill with respiratory infections resulting from constant exposure to horse manure, garbage, and human sewage that ran down the streets in the gutter. Whitman wrote about these men, who had names such as Broadway Jack, Dressmaker, Old Elephant and his brother Young Elephant, Pop Rice, and Patsy Dee, for the *New York Leader*: "There they are, many pining and wasting week after week with painful and incurable diseases—burning fevers, racking rheumatism, erysipelas, palsy, consumption, pneumonia, and all the long list; many brought in from sudden accidents, resulting in amputation, often followed by death." Whitman was a regular at the Broadway Hospital (at Pearl Street), where most of the injured or sick coach drivers in New York recuperated or died, and he was helpful and well liked by both the patients and the doctors, nurses, and staff. He was sympathetic and solicitous with all the patients he met, but "Uncle Walt" was always especially alert to the beautiful ones—the well built, the young, and the handsome, such as "poor James Watson," a twenty-six-year-old who'd been thrown from a train car in Jersey City and had a broken ankle and "a frightful wound," and who eventually died of a fever. Whitman was there when Watson was brought into the hospital, and he was there just before Watson wasted away and died, "three weeks ago a picture of athletic manly health, size and good looks."

Whitman's visits to the Broadway Hospital foreshadowed the years of the Civil War, when he would spend countless days and nights with wounded, sick, and dying soldiers, cheering them up, bringing them presents, and writing poignant letters to their parents, wives, and friends. His experiences, which he wrote about in *Memoranda During the War* and in a series of poems called *Drum-Taps*, were in turn a kind of precursor to similar experiences many gay men had in the 1980s and '90s when our friends and lovers were dying of AIDS.

The most moving passages of Whitman's *Memoranda*—for me, anyway—are the ones that bring to mind this recent plague of ours, and the days and nights many of us spent watching friends and lovers die. "I do not see that I do much good to these wounded and dying; but I cannot leave them. Once in a while some youngster holds on to me convulsively, and I do what I can for him; at any rate, stop with him and sit near him for hours, if he wishes it." At the height of the AIDS era, when the disease was so mysterious and untreatable, it sometimes seemed as if another kind of war was being waged, with

young gay men the unlikely soldiers. "I am more and more surprised at the very great proportion of youngsters . . . in the army," Whitman wrote. One boy, Charles Miller, Company D, Fifty-third Pennsylvania, "is only sixteen years of age, very bright, courageous boy, left leg amputated below the knee; next bed to him, another young lad very sick." Whitman's description of the atmosphere in army hospitals— primitive, unsanitary places in the 1860s—remind me of the atmosphere I remember from hospitals where I went to see my own dying friends: "You may hear groans or other sounds of unendurable suffering from two or three of the cots, but in the main there is quiet—almost a painful absence of demonstration; but the pallid face, the dull'd eye, and the moisture on the lip, are demonstration enough." In the same way as the soldiers did in the nineteenth century, many of the young men in hospital with AIDS showed signs of terribly recent physical fitness and beauty. "Look at the fine large frames, the bright and broad countenances, and the many yet lingering proofs of strong constitution and physique. Look at the patient and mute manner of our American wounded as they lie in such a sad collection; representatives from all New England, and from New York, and New Jersey, and Pennsylvania—indeed from all the States and all the cities. . . ."

Whitman tells of a soldier from Connecticut who could be a proud, rebellious, gay young man circa 1988: "Though not more than twenty-one, or thereabouts, he has knock'd much around the world, on sea and land, and he has seen some fighting on both. When I first saw him he was very sick, with no appetite. He declined offers of money—said he did not need anything."

And a soldier from New York has the same mad optimistic faith a friend of mine had on his deathbed when he was thirty-six.

This afternoon, July 22d, I have spent a long time with Oscar F. Wilber, company G, 154th New York, low with chronic diarrhea, and a bad wound also. He asked me to read him a chapter in the New Testament. I complied, and ask'd him what I should read. He said, "Make your own choice." I open'd at the close of one of the first books of the evangelists, and read the chapters describing the latter hours of Christ, and the scenes at the crucifixion. The poor, wasted young man ask'd me to read the following chapter also, how Christ rose again. I read very slowly, for Oscar was feeble. It pleased him very much, yet the tears were in his eyes. He ask'd me if I enjoyed religion. I said, "Perhaps not, my dear, in the way you mean, and yet, may-be, it is the same thing." He said, "It is my chief reliance." He talk'd of death, and said he did not fear it. I said, "Why, Oscar, don't you think you will get well?" He said, "I may, but it is not probable." . . . The kiss I gave him as I was about leaving he return'd fourfold. . . . He died a few days after the one just described.

I had another friend, Otis Stuart, who also had "knocked much around the world" by the time I knew him. He wrote a biography of Rudolf Nureyev, and I remember reading the proofs to him aloud, because his vision was nearly gone, and he was very weak—he was dying of AIDS. He was scheduled to read from the published book (his only one) in New York, but he was too sick to go the block and a half to the store, so his friends read aloud from the book instead. As I took my turn reading to the people gathered there that evening, I felt as if Otis could almost surely have heard my voice, his apartment was so nearby. He died within a week of the book's publication, having just managed to sign a single copy of it.

I used to sit with Otis in his apartment when he was sick and watch movies with him on the VCR. Once when I showed up, he was sitting on the floor, too weak to get up, the IV dangling into his arm. I don't know how long he had been there, but he just casually asked if I would help him up to his bed. I was trembling as I helped him up, hoping he wouldn't die there alone with me—I wasn't prepared for that at all.

The windows were always open in Otis's apartment, but somehow it was always stiflingly warm, and the smell of medicines and body fluids and soft foods was strong and sharp. It's strange that I should miss those frightening, sad days in Otis's stuffy, smelly apartment high above Seventh Avenue, but I do.

‹◇›

In 1890, when Whitman was seventy-one, he told a lie that's famous for its chutzpah and unbelievability. The English historian and critic John Addington Symonds had written to Whitman almost twenty years before, delicately requesting "some story of athletic friendship from which to learn the truth" about Whitman's sexuality. Symonds, who would continue to pose the question with increasing urgency and candidness in subsequent letters, probably hoped that since he, too, was gay, he and Whitman could enjoy a special bond if Whitman would confess to his own taboo desires. Instead, Whitman finally—absurdly—claimed to have fathered six children and to have had a "southern grandchild, fine boy" who still wrote letters to him. Of course Whitman may have been lying in a spirit of simple mischief and play; or he might have been trying seriously to dispel the idea that he was gay, for any number of reasons. In 1888, Whitman told his friend and biographer Horace Traubel that a letter from another gay Englishman, Edward Carpenter, made Carpenter "seem to be very close to his heart and he to mine." That letter from Carpenter, sent in 1874, reads in part:

Because you have, as it were, given me ground for the love of men, I thank you continually in my heart. (And others thank you though they do not say so.) For you have made men to be not ashamed of the noblest instinct of their nature. Women are beautiful; but to some, there is something that passes the love of women. It is enough to live wherever the divine beauty of love may flash on men; but indeed its real and enduring light seems infinitely far from us in this our day. Between the splendid dawn of Greek civilization and the high universal moon of Democracy there is a strange horror of darkness upon us.

Guessing about homosexual behavior in the nineteenth century is a mostly unprofitable business. There were people then, no doubt, doing most of the things homosexuals do now under the sign of sex. But figuring out *who* was doing *what* is where things get murky, because there are few records about such things in books, letters, or diaries. As far as we know, Whitman never committed anything detailed about his sex life to paper, though he did write some deeply suggestive poems and some pitiably beseeching love letters to boys. What is clear from much of Whitman's poetry and his *Memoranda During the War*, is that he was attracted—in every way—to the young soldiers he met during the Civil War.

"The actual soldier of 1862-'65, North and South," Whitman wrote at the end of his *Memoranda*, "with all his ways, his incredible dauntlessness, habits, practices, tastes, language, his fierce friendship, his appetite, rankness, his superb strength and animality, lawless gait, and a hundred unnamed lights and shades of camp, I say, will never be written—perhaps must not and should not be." Whitman's total experience with the Civil War soldiers, he knew, was not something he could ever convey in writing. Such feelings as he must have had so many times—of real, painful, hopeless love—for wounded or sick soldiers are not the kind that can be expressed with words, even by as great a poet as Whitman; but he tried. One of his last letters written to the parents of a dead solider was to the mother of Frank H. Irwin, Company E, Ninety-third Pennsylvania, who died May 1, 1865. This letter—one of Whitman's artless, beautiful masterpieces—evokes more poignantly than any of his poetry the brutality and the pathos of the war and, coincidentally, the pathos of our own years of battle, which, alas, are not over yet.

Dear madam: No doubt you and Frank's friends have heard the sad fact of his death in hospital here. . . . I will write you a few lines—as a casual friend that sat by his death-bed. Your son . . . was so good and well-behaved and affectionate, I myself liked him very much. I was in the habit of coming in afternoons and sitting by him, and soothing him, and he liked to have me—liked to put his arm out and lay his hand on my knee—would keep it so a long while. . . . He seem'd quite willing to die—he had become very weak and had suffer'd a good deal, and was perfectly resign'd, poor boy. I do not know his past life, but I feel as if it must have been good. At any rate what I saw of him here, under the most trying circumstances, with a painful wound, and among strangers, I can say that he behaved so brave, so composed, and so sweet and affectionate, it could not be surpass'd. And now like many other noble and good men, after serving his country as a soldier, he has yielded up his young life at the very outset in her service. Such things are gloomy—yet there is a text, "God doeth all things well"—the meaning of which, after due time, appears to the soul.

I thought perhaps a few words, though from a stranger, about your son, from one who was with him at the last, might be worth while—for I loved the young man, though I but saw him immediately to lose him. I am merely a friend visiting the hospitals occasionally to cheer the wounded and sick.

W. W.

ANOTHER OF AMERICA'S most influential writers was born in the same year as Whitman, 1819, and died just a year earlier, in 1891. His imagination, like Whitman's, was powerfully homoerotic, and he too, though in a key very different from Whitman's, sang a complex song of nineteenth-century America. Herman Melville was born on Pearl Street in New York City, the very downtown street where Whitman would later go to visit his wounded coachmen. Both New Yorkers, the two writers never met. Whitman came to be known as the happy bard; Melville as the unhappily married, struggling, unsuccessful, frustrated novelist whose greatest work, an enormous book about a man's religious devotion to his own triumph over the elements of nature as symbolized by a particular white whale, was recognized as one of the great novels of all time only some forty years after its author's death.

In 1849, two years before *Moby-Dick*, the thirty-year-old, already-married Melville composed, within a few summer months, what could fairly be considered the first great American gay novel, *Redburn: His First Voyage, Being the Sailor-boy Confessions and Reminiscences of the Son-of-a-Gentleman, in the Merchant Service*, a book Melville quickly came to scorn as "a thing, which I, the author, know to be trash." Considering why Melville insistently denounced such a charming, engaging book may shed some light on his stance toward his own sexuality: *Redburn* contains several scenes of powerfully erotic, all-male prose the likes of which had never been published by an American before.

It is also in *Redburn* that Melville pays homage to his father, who died when the author was thirteen. When the novel opens, Redburn's father is dead and there is a nostalgic yearning for the father's love throughout the text that speaks to a poignant craving for paternal love that is never met in a satisfactory or lasting way. This may be a familiar feeling for a lot of gay men (and for others as well). It has been my own experience with the man I believed for most of my life to be my father (I am actually in all probability a bastard love-child), and I found it deeply affecting to come across Melville's account of his young narrator's turbulent and difficult emotions for the father he misses and reveres and never got to know as intimately as he would have liked. After the novel had been published, Melville suggested a better subtitle for it: "a little nursery tale." Edwin Haviland Miller, in his biography of the writer, says, "In *Redburn* Melville wrote an In Memoriam to [his father], and, despite the merry tales of a bumpkin's adventures at sea, the comedy, as in *The Adventures of Huckleberry Finn*, is played out against an insistent death motif." That motif is kept in the background throughout most of *Redburn*, but it gives the whole story an impressive *gravitas* that it would otherwise lack.

<0>

Wellingborough Redburn, our young hero ("I was then but a boy," he says without specifying his age), is obliged to go to sea on account of his family's impoverished situation. He's a good kid, though his mother looks at him as he takes his leave in a way that makes him feel that perhaps he is after all "an erring and a willful boy"; but it "had been a hardhearted world, and hard times that had made" him that way. He leaves home depressed and bitter: "there is no misanthrope like a boy disappointed; and such was I, with the warm soul of me flogged out by adversity." He heads, in such a sorry state—disappointed by childhood like so many others before and after him—to New York City, from whence he'll depart for the wide, wide sea and some manly experience.

Aspects of style in *Redburn* were echoed a hundred years later in the similarly male-centric novels of Jean Genet, particularly by sentences giving expression to an ambiguous, hot mixture of momentary despair and pulsing promise. As Redburn leaves his hometown, he observes himself looking very much like one of Genet's tumescent bad boys: "The cold drops of drizzle trickled down my leather cap, and mingled with a few hot tears on my cheeks." Genet's lusty maritime novel *Querelle* opens with, "The notion of murder often brings to mind the notion of sea and sailors." Later in Genet's novel (his italics): *"My own cheeks still wet with tears, I revel in, and overflow with tenderness for the flat, hard cheekbones of those boys."* In both novels, a brothel and its employees are figures of both fascination and "repulsion."

Just getting to New York, 180 miles down the Hudson River, is nearly enough to drive the teenage Redburn to Querelle-like violence. Forced to sit on a ferryboat among a lot of unattractively loquacious and proper people, the painfully self-conscious Redburn has "the scent and savor of poverty" upon him, and he keeps to himself until the captain's clerk comes round for his ticket. Redburn has neither a ticket nor money enough to pay for one. He cheekily offers the clerk half the fare; the clerk takes it with a smart remark, leaving "every eye fastened upon" the embarrassed teenager. At the end of this humiliating little journey, he heads into the city, thoroughly if only temporarily demoralized, a well-known state of mind for almost all of Genet's painfully self-conscious, violently impetuous young men. Redburn laments:

I then turned on my heel, and shouldering my fowling-piece and bundle, marched on deck, and walked there through the dreary storm, till I was wet through, and the boat touched the wharf at New York.

Such is boyhood.

And so his boyhood ends. He sells his gun in a pawnshop for next to nothing, buys a red sweater and "two or three trifles," and throws his last penny into the ocean, which he immediately regrets.

The chapter headings in *Redburn* are perfect, plain descriptions of the essential action and mood of the story. Chapter Seven: "He Gets to Sea, and Feels Very Bad." Chapter Ten: "He is Very Much Frightened; the Sailors Abuse Him; and He Becomes Miserable and Forlorn."

In Chapter Twelve, "He Gives Some Account of One of His Shipmates Called Jackson," we meet one of Melville's most vividly immoral, nasty characters, for whom Redburn feels both overweening hatred and an irrepressible respect and sympathy. Considered by himself and everyone on board to be the ablest seaman on the ship, Jackson is a bitter bully, a snarling, cussing, spitting creature who is also the cleverest and the best educated of all the men aboard save the captain. "It was impossible to tell how old this Jackson was; for he had no beard, and no wrinkles, except small crows-feet about the eyes. He might have seen thirty, or perhaps fifty years. But according to his own account, he had been to sea ever since he was eight years old, when he first went as a cabin-boy in an Indiaman, and ran away at Calcutta. And according to his own account, too, he had passed through every kind of dissipation and abandonment in the worst parts of the world." Everything he talked of was "full of piracies, plagues and poisonings." Jackson had, according to himself, earned the right to treat everyone else on board badly, and to work only when he was inspired to. "He was a horrid desperado; and like a wild Indian, whom he resembled in his tawny skin and high cheek bones, he seemed to run a muck at heaven and earth. He was a Cain afloat; branded on his yellow skin with some inscrutable curse; and going about corrupting and searing every heart that beat near him." Redburn watches Jackson carefully during their journey aboard the *Highlander* to Liverpool; and he sees him die on the return trip, spewing blood from atop a high mast during a gale, just off the shore of Cape Cod, and plummeting into the ocean.

Redburn tries to enjoy his new life on the ship, and to think of it in romantic, epic terms. He appreciates his first profound experience of being away from land. What "seemed perhaps the most strange to me of all, was a certain wonderful rising and falling of the sea; I do not mean the waves themselves, but a sort of wide heaving and swelling and sinking all over the ocean. It was something I can not very well describe; but I know very well what it was, and how it affected me." I'm reminded by this of an experience I had many times during my childhood, and a few times since. The first time it happened, I had walked in my sleep to a sofa situated between the bedroom I shared with my brother and the bedroom shared by my parents. It must have been very late; the house was silent and dark. I sat up on the edge of the sofa and felt a sort of heaviness in my limbs and a kind of pressure bearing down on me from above, and a heaving, rising and falling motion about it all that was subtle and slow and, I felt, very profound. It changed me in some vaguely spiritual way; in a way, I'd like to think, similar to the way the sea changed Redburn. "I felt," writes Melville, "as if in a dream all the time; and when I could shut the ship out, almost thought I was in some new, fairy world, and expected to hear myself called to, out of the clear blue air, or from the depths of the deep blue sea."

Redburn learns quickly and he gets along well enough as a "boy" on his first voyage. (Though biographers have shown that the novel is generally autobiographical, they have also confirmed that Melville was actually twenty, not a teenager, when he made his first voyage on a ship.) He makes the acquaintance of all the men on board, including the cook, Mr. Thompson, and his friend the steward, a "handsome, dandy mulatto, that had once been a barber in West-Broadway, [who] went by the name of Lavender" and wore a turban over his "uncommon head of frizzled hair" which he kept "well perfumed with Cologne water, of which he had a large supply, the relics of his West-Broadway stock in trade." This gorgeous fellow, who wore "claret-colored suits, and snuff-colored suits, and red velvet vests, and buff and brimstone pantaloons" along with "an uncommon large pursy ring on his fore-finger, with something he called a real diamond in it," spent every fine evening with Mr. Thompson, the cook. They would "sit on the little shelf in the cook-house, leaning up against each other" until "after dark, smoking their pipes and gossiping." Mr. Thompson would take out his Bible some nights and work toward the salvation of Lavender, "whom he knew to be a sad profligate and gay deceiver ashore; addicted to every youthful indiscretion." Lavender would pay close, respectful attention to these readings and impromptu sermons, but "he was a wicked youth, he knew it—he had broken a good many hearts, and many eyes were weeping for him even then, both in New York, and Liverpool, and London, and Havre. But how could he help it? He hadn't made his handsome face, and fine head of hair, and graceful figure. It was not *he*, but the others, that were to blame; for his bewitching person turned all heads and subdued all hearts, wherever he went." And not just the heads and hearts of the ladies, clearly.

Chapter Fifteen: "The Melancholy State of His Wardrobe," in which we find a long, loving paragraph about our narrator's splendid boots, which he had earlier liked to gaze upon while in church. They had "very high heels" and the long legs of them, coming almost to the knee, were "mounted with red morocco." Looking almost unrecognizable by the time he gets home again, they were "almost new" when he left. He loved them. "In a word," he says, sounding like something of a dandy himself, "they were a beautiful pair of boots."

The trip to Liverpool is smooth and interesting, and Redburn disports himself well as a sailor boy. He gets used to climbing up the high masts with a heavy bucket of water (and learns never to call it a pail). His nerves become "as steady as the earth's diameter."

‹◊›

A six-year-old English boy, "not four feet high," suddenly appears one day aboard the ship, to everyone's amazement. The son of an English carpenter and widower who'd gone to New York and died there, the boy wanted to go home to England and had sneaked onto the ship. The captain gives him a stern talking-to and sends him down to live among the sailors, who "received him with open arms; but before caressing him much, they gave him a thorough washing in the lee-scuppers, when he turned out to be quite a handsome lad, though thin and pale with the hardships he had suffered. However, by good nursing and plenty to eat, he soon improved and grew fat; and before many days was as fine a looking little fellow, as you might pick out of Queen Victoria's nursery.

"The sailors took the warmest interest in him. One made him a little hat with a long ribbon. . . ." Eventually, his fate ashore unknown to everyone, he disappears into the crowd in Liverpool, having enjoyed the voyage as the favorite of all the sailors except Jackson, the despised and despising bully who, stung by the boy's reluctance to come near him, "seemed to hate [the boy], harmless as he was, along with all the rest of the world."

In preparation for the six weeks they'll spend in Liverpool—in England, an actual foreign country—Redburn eagerly peruses the guidebook his father used when *he* visited the same city, a book the boy already knows well. "As I now linger over the volume, to and fro turning the pages so dear to my boyhood,—the very pages which, years and years ago, my father turned over amid the very scenes that are here described; what a soft, pleasing sadness steals over me, and how I melt into the past and forgotten!" He comes upon some notes his father made on certain pages of the book about his itinerary and expenses. These notes "are full of a strange, subdued, old, midsummer interest to me." He follows along his father's movements and interests. "By these marks, I perceive that my father forgot not his religion in a foreign land; but attended St. John's Church near the Hay-market...." Redburn intends to make a "filial pilgrimage," retracing his father's steps in the city; but he finds that everything has changed, or so it seems; everything in Liverpool—in all of England—appears to have become darker, more dangerous, and more mysterious. The old guidebook is of almost no use at all: "the thing that had guided the father, could not guide the son. And I sat down on a shop step, and gave loose to meditation." He rises, a while later, "a sadder and wiser boy."

Redburn reluctantly gives up on the past, and settles in to seeing the present, making the acquaintance of all sorts of people, none of whom could be described as powerfully attractive to the bewildered boy until he meets Harry Bolton, "a handsome, accomplished, but unfortunate youth" with "curling hair, and silken muscles.... His complexion was a mantling brunette, feminine as a girl's; his feet were small; his hands were white; and his eyes were large, black, and womanly; and, poetry aside, his voice was as the sound of a harp." After spotting him on several evenings "standing in doorways," Redburn approaches him and they become, for a while, inseparable friends. Harry tells the story of his past—an orphan, the heir to an aunt's small fortune, which he gambled away in London one winter, now he's a wandering waif, although certainly not a child. "There was a dash of romance in it; a taking abandonment; and a scorn of fine coats, which exactly harmonized with his reckless contempt, at the time, for all past conventionalities." Redburn had found a "comrade," Walt Whitman's favorite word; "he shared with me his purse and his heart." They would recline "side by side in some agreeable nook" of an afternoon, and stroll together arm-in-arm, and talk. Harry boasts of his high life in London—he gives Redburn "the measurement of Madame Vestris' ankle" and makes "various but enigmatical allusions to a certain Lady Georgiana Theresa, the noble daughter of an anonymous earl." Redburn finds all this fascinating, of course, but it also makes him uncomfortable, taking it as he does as evidence of the separating differences between his own limited experience and Harry's, so much wider and worldlier, which "made me hold back my whole soul from him; when, in its loneliness, it was yearning to throw itself into the unbounded bosom of some immaculate friend."

But immaculate Harry is not. Learning of Redburn's desire to see London, he makes a few arrangements and off they go. Once in the great city, instead of showing Redburn Westminster Abbey and the Parliament, Harry insists that they go directly to a bizarre house that gets stranger the longer they stay, which is just long enough for Harry to disappear for the night. The house, No. 40, the one with the purple light, is full of men, exclusively. "It was some semi-public place of opulent entertainment" called "Aladdin's Palace" in which the most beguiling things appear to be going on while Redburn sits alone in an empty, luxurious room. "And all the while, Harry ran through my soul—in and out, at every door, that burst open to his vehement rush."

Redburn, having survived the night that Harry seems thoroughly to have enjoyed among the men at Aladdin's Palace, goes back to Liverpool with Harry just in time to board the ship back to America. Redburn once again "a sadder and wiser boy."

‹◊›

The return voyage is a harrowing battle with weather and plague and a lack of food that puts an end to many of the emigrant passengers who desperately paid to board the ship. Redburn witnesses several dozen burials at sea, and he watches Jackson die; he sees vivid instances of avarice and selfishness, grief and loneliness, and muted joy. "But as the dying departed, the places of two of them were filled in the rolls of humanity, by the birth of two infants, whom the plague, panic, and gale had hurried into the world before their time. The first cry of one of these infants, was almost simultaneous with the splash of its father's body in the sea. Thus we come and go."

The only relief on the voyage home comes from Carlo, a beautiful "rich-cheeked, chestnut-haired Italian boy," fifteen years old and the proud owner of an extraordinary organ with which he manages to distract and entertain nearly everyone on the ship. He apparently made upon the author a very memorable impression: "in the twilight pensiveness of his full morning eyes, there seemed to sleep experiences so sad and various, that his days must have seemed to him years." Whereas Harry's eye had been "large and womanly," Carlo's "shone

with a soft and spiritual radiance, like a moist star in a tropic sky; and spoke of humility, deep-seated thoughtfulness, yet a careless endurance of all the ills of life." He was "such a boy as gipsies steal in infancy"; he could sing more amazingly than anyone Redburn had ever had the pleasure of hearing. And then there was the matter of his wonderful organ. "What sculptured arches, leading into mysterious intricacies!" Redburn watches closely as young Carlo plays for the pleasure of the sailors: ". . . as Carlo now turns his hand, I hear the gush of the Fountain of Lions, as he plays some thronged Italian air—a mixed and liquid sea of sound, that dashes its spray in my face.

"Play on, play on, Italian boy! . . . whilst I list to the organs twain— one yours, one mine—let me gaze fathoms down into thy fathomless eye;—'tis good as gazing down into the great South Sea. . . ."

Carlo, with his enchanting organ and soprano voice, had absolute control over Redburn and many of the others. They were powerless before Carlo's awesome skill. Carlo's music—was it just his music?— could send Redburn into deep reveries and hallucinations. "All this could Carlo do—make, unmake me; build me up; to pieces take me; and join me limb to limb. He is the architect of domes of sound, and bowers of song."

A lovelier gay love song was never written in American prose before, and none lovelier than this chapter of *Redburn* has been written since. How appropriate that Carlo, when the ship comes in to New York, is rowed ashore only in order to disappear (like the stow-away boy after arriving home in England), having paid his way with his music and his charm, "seated in the stern of the boat, his organ before him, and something like 'Hail Columbia!' his tune. We gave him three rapturous cheers and we never saw Carlo again."

After a short interval, Redburn also loses track of Harry Bolton. The last he hears of the young man is of his death years later off the coast of Brazil. He'd been on a whaling boat whose crew was lost while "chasing a whale after sundown."

‹◊›

Redburn was written in a kind of gorgeous code. It seems very likely to us now, judging from all that we know of Melville the man, that he had an imagined or even preconscious erotic life he was not able or willing to realize or consummate in a satisfying way. His style as a writer reflected, like a mirror, his longing, aching, searching drives and feelings; when we read a text as plangently autobiographical as *Redburn*, we can sense the author—the young Melville—examining himself and looking, amidst the chaos and confusion of circumstance, for the way to live. Harry Bolton—whatever his name was in real life—must have represented one possibility, one kind of life, for the young Melville. In her beautiful brief biography of Melville, Elizabeth Hardwick writes, "Harry Bolton is lifelike as a certain type of frenzied, melodramatic homosexual down on his luck, and as such he is as embarrassing and interesting as life itself. . . . He is a stranger, an English youth, fluent in self-creation." When Melville, speaking as Redburn, says that he never saw the beautiful Carlo again, and when he loses track of Harry, he seems to be expressing the heartbreaking admission that there were such losses for him, too—for Melville himself—that proved permanent; these losses, in the novel, seem to have involved more than the simple loss of casual gay friends. Melville apparently got separated, as he grew into adulthood, from the sort of sensual realization of his sexuality that he envisions in *Redburn*.

As fluent in the creation of literary art as anyone ever has been, Melville created himself early on, partly in the form of *Redburn*; and a version of him seems to have disappeared, like Carlo and Harry and the mysterious English boy, without spending enough time in one place to be understood or loved for long.

THE TROUBADOURS, in the south of France, were some of the finest lyric poets of all time. They wrote and performed, for a courtly audience, songs that were mostly about the search for a lasting, sustaining happiness through the instrumentality of love. The object of the troubadour's passionate love was usually an inaccessible, upper-class, indifferent woman who gave the poor poet little if any attention, which caused the poet to suffer accordingly—his passion was painful, and his poems were among the first in the history of the Western world to say so. The troubadours perfected stylized suffering from love as we have known it for nine hundred years—it is to them and their songs (the few that have survived) that historians look for some of the very first recorded expressions, in any form, of a passionate, complex love for a particular person. Denis de Rougemont writes in *Love in the Western World*: "The West is distinct from other cultures not only by its invention of passionate love in the twelfth century and the secular elaboration of conjugal love, but by its confusion of the notions of eros, agape, sexuality, passion." The love of the troubadour for his lady contained the poet's passion, his sex, his kindness, and his vision of what life should be in its highest, most radiant manifestation.

Bernart de Ventadorn, who wrote in the years 1150-1180, was among the most refined of the troubadours. His songs are dramatic lyrics that often express his conviction that if the woman he loves does not deign to recognize him as a worthy admirer, he will surely die—or at least suffer excruciatingly and at length. While Bernart clearly intended an ironic effect, his songs have a beautifully sincere and heartfelt pathos.

> In good faith and without deceit
> Do I love the best and most beautiful lady.
> I sigh from my heart and weep tears from my eyes
> Because I love her so much that it hurts.
> What more can I do, if Love takes hold of me
> And the only key that will open the prison
> Love has put me in is pity,
> And I find no pity in her?

> This love wounds my heart
> With a sweet delight:
> I die of grief a hundred times a day
> And a hundred times revive with joy.
> My pain seems beautiful,
> It is worth more than any pleasure;
> And if even my pain is pleasing to me,
> How good the happiness will be after the suffering is over.

The troubadours dreamt and sang (in Provençal) of *fin amors*, a "refining and purifying love" that brings self-improvement and may ultimately (if ever consummated) bring the lover peace of mind and lasting happiness. This "distant" type of love was very different from the more common, more carnal love most ordinary people enjoy, which according to the troubadours usually makes its victims unhappy, jealous, and anxious, however pleasurable it may be for a while. A degree of suffering is also built into *fin amors*, however, since the lover cannot expect satisfaction anytime soon. According to L. T. Topsfield, author of the sublime 1975 study *Troubadours and Love*, "The framework of love is fixed by social formalities, but Bernart's lyric genius is anything but social or formal. To situations that demand mannered elegance he reacts with impassioned poetic feeling and the seeming artlessness of direct and largely monosyllabic poetic language." Bernart's songs were early examples in what became a long history (one still very much alive today in popular music) of poets and songwriters addressing their beloved directly— in language at once tormented, ravished, and adoring—about their nearly unbearable situation of being exquisitely in love and achingly unsatisfied by the insufficient attention of the beloved.

It came as a pleasant surprise, years after I had read the troubadours' poems, to find an echo of them in some letters by an American poet I also loved. Some seven centuries after Bernart, and far from the south of France, the spirit of troubadour poetry enjoyed a private, unlikely renaissance in Amherst, Massachusetts. It was not so much in Emily Dickinson's poetry that this uncanny resemblance is to be found—her poetry is utterly unlike any others'—but in the very passionate early love letters she wrote to her future sister-in-law Susan.

<>

Emily Dickinson (1830–1886) wrote more letters to Susan Huntington Gilbert (later Dickinson) during the course of her life than to anyone else, even though for thirty years Susan was the reclusive poet's next-door neighbor. Over 250 letters from Emily to Susan survive. There were also letters from Emily to Susan that have been lost—the ones Susan judged "too personal and adulatory ever to be printed."

But the letters we do know of constitute an important secondary body of the great poet's literary work.

The first twenty-two of the surviving letters from Emily to Susan, mostly in prose, express a powerful love that cannot be dismissed as merely the enthusiastic attentions of an adolescent playing a conventional role in a popular nineteenth-century cult of girlish affections. Susan's daughter, Martha Dickinson Bianchi, wrote about her aunt in a 1915 essay for the *Atlantic Monthly*: "Her devotion to those she loved was that of a knight for his lady." And Emily herself once wrote, in a letter to Susan, that "chivalry" was to her "a shining Word." Emily's earliest letters to Susan give an impression very much like that of a courtly poet eloquently, forlornly wooing his lady, using an eccentric syntax and a pained, impassioned language.

> It's a sorrowful morning Susie—the wind blows and it rains; "into each life some rain must fall," and I hardly know which falls fastest, the rain without, or within—Oh Susie, I would nestle close to your warm heart, and never hear the wind blow, or the storm beat, again. Is there any room for me, or shall I wander away all homeless and alone?

Dickinson's wishful plaint is very much like any number of Bernart's dimly hopeful songs. Bernart identifies with natural things that pass inevitably away because he has begun to believe that he, too, will expire soon—not from any of the usual causes, but from lack of love. He *almost* accepts the apparent indifference of his lady, and he considers giving up (in despair), but something he is unable to name—perhaps his own obsessive personality—ties him to her permanently and helplessly.

When I see the leaves
Falling down from the trees,
Which may upset someone else,
It suits me very well.
Don't believe that I want
To see a mere flower or leaf—
The one I want most
Is cold with pride.
I have the heart to break away
But not the strength—
Because I always think, when I most despair,
That perhaps she'll receive me yet.

The theme of the beloved *about to submit*—perhaps—to the lover's poetic pleas became among the most prominent in the private life of Emily Dickinson and particularly in her lifelong (and probably unconsummated) love affair with her sister-in-law.

‹◊›

Emily and Susan were born nine days apart in December 1830, and by their late teens they were close friends. The two girls came from very different backgrounds: Emily's family was, compared to Susan's, quite rich and distinguished. Edward Dickinson was a congressman. Susan was an orphan at age eleven and did housework to earn her keep. But she had an older brother, Frank, who became a millionaire banker; he was generous with her, and she was sent to Amherst Academy, a good school near Mount Holyoke, where Emily was studying.

When they met, the two girls were unusually sensitive and passionate, and they both felt themselves to be in need of mothering:

The First Time I Met Frank O'Hara

Susan's mother was long dead (she died when Susan was seven), and Emily felt that she herself "never had a mother" due to her mother's simple, retiring, submissive nature. At nineteen, Susan wrote to her brother: "I do feel so lonely at times dear brother, I feel so keenly the loss of a mother's love, and influence, and that sympathy our Mother alone could give." It didn't take the two girls long to see in each other an attentive, comforting, intimate friend, and Emily's first letters to Susan begin a long story of love that is never fully requited—a distant love in which Emily plays the lowly, suffering poet and Susan the aristocratic lady, a reversal of their early real-life social positions that would endure for both their lifetimes. Here's Emily to Susan in 1852, when both were twenty-one:

> Do I repine, is it all murmuring, or am I sad and lone, and cannot, cannot help it? Sometimes when I do feel so, I think it may be wrong, and that God will punish me by taking you away; for he is very kind to let me write to you, and to give me your sweet letters, but my heart wants <u>more</u>.

A year later Susan agreed, without enthusiasm, to marry Emily's brother Austin. He was aware, more or less immediately, of a coldness in his fiancée, particularly concerning the prospect of sexual intimacy between them. He assured her, though, that she would not be forced to live in any wise other than "as a girl" if she wished it so—and he eventually had affairs with other women to make up for his wife's lack of sexual passion with him. But Austin was clearly in love, and he courted Susan for years. Finally, after she recovered from a yearlong, mysterious "illness" (indecisiveness? anxious hysteria?), they were married on July 1, 1856. In a letter to her brother, who'd been strangely silent on the subject, written just prior to her marriage, Susan says: "Why don't you write to me Frank and congratulate me, that I have found someone who is going, by and by, to encumber himself with me?" In the same letter, she refers to her future husband as her "companion," a poor young man who will not be able to give her all the "enjoyments that wealth could procure, and that no one loves more than I," but she agrees to forego those things in order to have a "cozy place" where her brothers and sisters can come to visit. It is not a letter brimming with romantic sentiment, to say the least. Susan was socially ambitious, and she knew very well that she was marrying the son of a wealthy man who would almost certainly be rich himself; their first house was a large Italianate villa called Evergreens, the first house in Amherst to bear a name. Her report of the wedding itself is equally cool: "a little cake—a little ice cream and it is all over—the millionth wedding since the world began."

Emily Dickinson seems to have fallen in love with Susan very early, and her love—though it climaxed, along with her productivity as a poet, in the early 1860s—remained passionate on her side until the end of her life. She loved Susan's energy and vitality, her ambition and intelligence and resistance to sentimentality. A year before Susan agreed to marry Austin, Emily wrote to her:

> ... How dull our lives must seem to the bride, and the plighted maiden, whose days are fed with gold, and who gather pearls every evening; but to the <u>wife</u>, Susie, sometimes the <u>wife forgotten</u>, our lives perhaps seem dearer than all others in the world; you have seen the flowers at morning, <u>satisfied</u> with the dew, and those same sweet flowers at noon with their heads bowed in anguish before the mighty sun; think you these thirsty

blossoms will <u>now</u> need naught but—<u>dew</u>? No, they will cry for sunlight, and pine for the burning noon, tho' it scorches them, scathes them; they have got through with peace—they know that the man of noon, is <u>mightier</u> than the morning and their life is henceforth to him. Oh, Susie, it is dangerous, and it is all too dear, these simple trusting spirits, and the spirits mightier, which we cannot resist! It does so rend me, Susie, the thought of it when it comes, that I tremble lest at sometime I, too, am yielded up.

Susie, you will forgive me my amatory strain—it has been a very long one, and if this saucy page did not here bind and fetter me, I might have had no end. . . .

This letter (excerpted here) was written in June 1852, at the end of a long year (long for Emily, at least) during which Susan was in Baltimore, teaching in a school for girls. She was about to return to Amherst, where both Emily and Austin Dickinson would continue to pursue her simultaneously. This is the letter containing Emily's most direct argument for the two women to shun the conventions of heterosexuality and marriage; though she does not make any overt proposal, the letter harbors a romantic rhetoric that is clearly meant to persuade Susan of *something*, some form of action. She suggests that although the "man of noon" is "mightier" than "the morning," the most "simple trusting spirits" could conceivably resist the powerful myth of the usual kind of domestic happiness. Emily has already made up her mind: she will not give up her morning dream of satisfaction and ecstasy. She knows—or believes she knows—what makes *her* happy. But she also implicitly and sadly acknowledges that, for Susan, a life of lesbian seclusion with Emily is probably not feasible or even desirable. Susan, who has no genius to fall back on as Emily

does, would be seen—and would see herself—as little more than a poor spinster if she chose not to marry. It's impossible to know what her true sexual inclinations were, or what really went on between her and Emily—few of *her* letters to Emily have survived—but she married Austin and gave birth to three children, settling in next door to Emily where she could be safely adored and loved by her brilliant but eccentric sister-in-law with no unseemliness or loss of social status or material comfort.

The First Time I Met Frank O'Hara

By June 27, Susan was still not back in Amherst and Emily was apparently nearly mad with desire. Susan was expected finally to arrive the first Saturday in July. "Susie," Emily urgently writes, "will you indeed come home next Saturday, and be my own again, and kiss me as you used to?" Emily was acutely distracted by her wish to be reunited with Susan, and again her language is similar to that of the troubadour pining away for a glimpse of his lady, who is always about to appear. "I hope for you so much," Emily writes in the same letter, "and feel so eager for you, feel that I <u>cannot</u> wait, feel that <u>now</u> I must have you— that the expectation once more to see your face again, makes me feel hot and feverish, and my heart beats so fast—I go to sleep at night, and the first thing I know, I am sitting there wide awake, and clasping my hands tightly, and thinking of next Saturday, and 'never a bit' of you." Emily sitting up wide awake in bed in the night, undone by the anticipation of seeing Susan again soon is reminiscent of Bernart in the middle of the twelfth century tossing and turning in the anxiety of his hallucinogenic passion for his own unresponsive lady:

> I don't know where to take cover
> From the sad thoughts that pull me down.
> The whole night long I toss and turn
> On the edge of my bed.
> I bear more pain from love
> Than Tristan the lover,
> Who suffered many sorrows
> For the fair Isolde.

By the mid-1850s, Emily had begun to accept Susan's gradual decision to marry Austin and live as a married woman, though not without some dramatic moments of emotional protest. The following letter, which is the first of the letters to Susan to close with a full-scale, mature poem, was written when both women were twenty-four: certainly this one, at least, must count as the considered thoughts of one grown woman to another. Emily, once again echoing the poetry of the troubadours, tried to rein herself in (to stay within the limits of what the troubadours called *mesura*, a crucial word in their lexicon referring to "the mean between too much and too little") while at the same time expressing her genuine grief over the fact that Susan would never "belong" to her.

> Sue—you can go or stay—There is but one alternative—We differ often lately, and this must be the last.
>
> You need not fear to leave me lest I should be alone, for I often part with things I fancy I have loved, —sometimes to the grave, and sometimes to an oblivion rather bitterer than death—thus my heart bleeds so frequently that I shant mind the hemorrhage, and I only add an agony to several previous ones, and at the end of day remark—a bubble burst!
>
> Such incidents would grieve me when I was but a child, and perhaps I could have wept when little feet hard by mine, stood still in the coffin, but eyes grow dry sometimes, and hearts get crisp and cinder, and had as lief burn.
>
> Sue—I have lived by this. . . .

Emily then, in this same astonishing letter, suggested that an image even more powerful than that of heaven inhabited her mind, a "darker spirit" upon which she had come irresistibly to rely—something, presumably, to do with her power as a poet. Emily here followed directly in the path of medieval philosophers, the spiritual fathers of the troubadour poets, who wrote of three types of human experience: the sensual, the imaginary, and the visionary. For the troubadours, lasting happiness was to be found only at the top of this hierarchy of concepts, beginning with the sensual and mounting up to the imaginary and finally to the visionary. In one of Emily's last surviving prose letters to Susan, the beginning of which is quoted above, she achieved a kind of original, visionary intensity:

> It is the lingering emblem of the Heaven I once dreamed, and though if this is taken, I shall remain alone, and though in that last day, the Jesus Christ you love, remark he does not know me—there is a darker spirit will not disown its child.
>
> Few have been given me, and if I love them so, that for <u>idolatry</u>, they are removed from me—I simply murmur <u>gone</u>, and the billow dies away into the boundless blue, and no one knows but me, that one went down today. We have walked very pleasantly—Perhaps this is the point at which our paths diverge—then pass on singing Sue, and up the distant hill I journey on.

〈◇〉

Susan was loyal to Emily as a friend until the end of the poet's life and beyond: it was she who tended to Emily as the poet lay dying, and she wrote Emily's obituary, printed in the *Springfield Republican*. In the beautiful two-page article, Susan associates Emily with the milieu of hothouse horticulture, an atmosphere that seems pertinent to the warm relations the two women enjoyed with each other for so many years: ". . . her gentle tillage of the rare flowers filling her conservatory, into which, as into the heavenly Paradise, entered nothing that could defile, and which was ever abloom in frost or sunshine, so well she knew her subtle chemistries. . . ."

All we know about the relationship between Emily and Susan is what we can find in the letters and poems that survive, along with a few other biographical traces. The letters from Emily to Susan alone, however, give us ample evidence of feelings engaged in ways that either woman was unlikely ever to experience again, or with another. Emily eventually developed, in a much more measured way, affectionate feelings for a man (Samuel Bowles), and Susan remained married to the unfaithful Austin, but never again did Emily sing such a passionate, painfully bereft, sublime lovesong as the one that ends the spectacular letter from the mid-1850s to her not-yet-married best friend:

> I have a Bird in spring
> Which for myself doth sing—
> The spring decoys.
> And as the summer nears—
> And as the Rose appears,
> Robin is gone.
>
> Yet do I not repine
> Knowing that Bird of mine
> Though flown—
> Learneth beyond the sea
> Melody new for me
> And will return.
>
> Fast in a safer hand
> Held in a truer Land

The First Time I Met Frank O'Hara

Are mine—
And though they now depart,
Tell I my doubting heart
They're thine.

In a serener Bright,
In a more golden light
I see
Each little doubt and fear,
Each little discord here
Removed.

Then will I not repine,
Knowing that Bird of mine
Though flown
Shall in a distant tree
Bright melody for me
Return.
                  E—

The Gay Century

DURING THE TWENTIETH CENTURY, a subculture came to life—and eventually died out—that we can think of as a gay culture. By gay culture I mean all of the ideas, traditions, gestures, art, and style that sprang from the resistance of gay men and women to the oppression they felt from a society that was contemptuous, fearful, and suspicious of those people who threatened the sexual ideals and fantasies of "normalcy" cherished by the mainstream. Gay culture, which put gay people *as gay people* in full possession of their unique intellectual, personal, and artistic capabilities and powers, is now a thing of the past, though there are still traces and reminders of it in certain quarters of all Western cities of any considerable size. Gay people are no longer in the same boat with the truly oppressed— we have swum ashore, with help from the landlubbers. Which is not to suggest that homophobia has disappeared—it probably never will; forms of hatred are notably durable and adaptable.

There have, of course, been people predisposed to varieties of same-sex erotic behavior since at least antiquity; but never before had anyone lived in a time and place that could have been reasonably thought of as fostering and benefiting from a gay culture. And though it is currently in abeyance, due to the triumph of gay liberation, stranger things have happened than an unexpected setback for that liberation and an attendant revival of gay culture. Gay culture wasted quickly away along with what sometimes seemed to be an entire generation of creative gay men in the mid-1980s and '90s—roughly the decade when I was in my twenties and living mostly in New York City (as I do again now). The struggle that gave gay culture its energy and justification is over and evidently, as history has shown, a subculture cannot thrive without the energizing momentum that comes from a group of people fighting for the right to be free. Once a degree of liberation is achieved, the culture that sprang up from that struggle tends toward the mainstream—always a culture of mediocrity.

‹◊›

The most prescient of late nineteenth-century gay writers in terms of the creation of a gay culture was the Anglo-Irish genius Oscar Wilde (1854-1900). His work as playwright, novelist, aphorist, journalist, lecturer, Socialist, and particularly as essayist, gave gay culture the impetus and direction it would take off and evolve from for the next hundred years.

It was neglect of the first of Wilde's monumental 1894 "Phrases and Philosophies for the Use of the Young" that precipitated the recent downfall of gay culture: "The first duty in life is to be as artificial as possible." A whole book—a whole life—could be composed on this theme alone; its implications are countless and endlessly conducive to robust gay philosophy. Consider some of the attitudes and habits this provocative phrase sets itself *against*: an easy relation to nature, an acceptance of inherited traits (including "the body one was born with"), a tendency to speak the first words that come to mind, a preoccupation with "organic" beauty. More positively, Wilde's injunction advises us to cultivate a life surrounded by design, wit, and the infinite varieties of things and people and ideas that have been honed and perfected in order to give, above all else, a noticeable *effect*. "Where the cultured catch an effect," Wilde wrote, describing an oil painting showing a London fog, "the uncultured catch cold."

Another of Wilde's crucial prescriptions for gay culture: "Pleasure is the only thing one should live for. Nothing ages like happiness." Along the same lines, and likewise admonitory against twelve-hour days and dreary full-time jobs: "Industry is the root of all ugliness." Another motto, this one pertinent to the historical illegality of homosexual acts and the often justified reputation homosexuals have long had for vice and lawlessness as well as high-mindedness (of the ironic type): "No crime is vulgar, but all vulgarity is crime." Another, pertaining to everyone: "One should either be a work of art, or wear a work of art."

The underlying principle of Wilde's wit was metaphysical, intended to comment on the *ultimate* conditions in which we live. The principle is simply this, from "The Decay of Lying" (1889): "Truth is entirely and absolutely a matter of style." The whole spectacle of gay culture developed not so much from the idea that the style with which a person presented himself to the world had priority over the person's actual thoughts, as from the notion that his substance and his style were identical. A person living within gay culture was (ideally) immune to ordinary impulses; his refined instincts were always for the extravagant. Such was the nature of his passions and his loves and enthusiasms; he always sought the highest plane upon which to move through life. A gay man in a gay culture didn't merely dream about a lovely life; he lived one, if necessary on next to no money.

Gay culture was, among other things, an heroic attempt at giving beauty a privileged status in everyday life rather than settling for its more expected, arranged appearances in predictable places such as museums, gardens, and fashion magazines. Gay culture's guiding light was the superstitious (but wonderful) belief that beauty is good *per se*, and that unusual exposure to and appreciation of beauty in all of its various manifestations will bestow upon a person a kind of blessing, which in its oldest meaning is the good fortune of *more life*, both in time and in terms of vitality and energy.

But none of this should be considered for long without taking note of Wilde's proviso that "Thought is wonderful, but adventure is more wonderful still." The main point is that where there is no style, there is no truth, and "Where there is no extravagance, there is no love."

‹◊›

"If you wish to understand others," Wilde said, "you must intensify your own individualism." Everyone in a gay culture strives to be unique in a particular, emphatic way; and to understand him or her (or anyone else), it's necessary to have your own experience of uniqueness. Everyone in a gay culture also feels himself or herself to be, to some extent, outside the family—outside the enfolding circle. It is this feeling of estrangement (and it's not only gay people, of course, that feel sometimes estranged) that makes possible an unusually deep understanding of other people. Nowadays, when most people feel much less estranged than in the past, it's less common for us to have a complex, rich, enthusiastic understanding of other people. We appear to each other now as foreign and unknowable, intractably apart, but at the same time as very much like everyone else.

It's not a tragedy that gay culture is gone—the world was perhaps improved by its influence, and in any case traces of it (like traces of any culture that once thrived) will always remain with us—but it was a tragedy that brought about its end. Now that the plague of AIDS is turning into something more like another cause of death in America along with cancer, heart disease, and suicide, and gay people have by various means become just another minority in a world without much of a

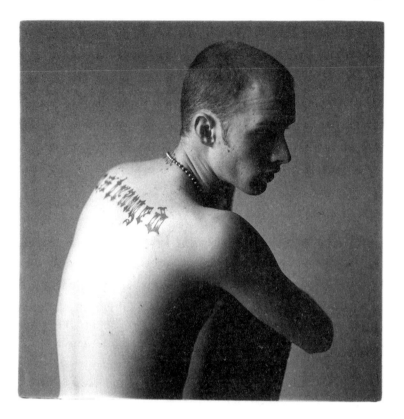

majority, the drive to understand other people has been transformed into a drive to be *like* other people. When the world saw gay men by the hundreds of thousands drop dead like so many soldiers on the home front, ordinary homophobic people in many parts of the world suddenly lacked the courage of their old conviction that homosexuals were sinners and perverted, inverted freakish weaklings worthy only of being despised. Through sympathy, gay people particularly in the United States won a wholesome place fully within the middle-class, corporate-driven, capitalistic society we once shunned and were shunned by, and we've never looked back or asked ourselves if that's really where we want to be. The cost of losing gay culture has been accepted as a reasonable price for the promise of a good life in a democratic and civilized world where bigotry and "hate crimes," in their most blatant manifestations, are not tolerated. Improvements in the treatment of AIDS seemed, for a while, to come along on an almost daily basis; it was a curious coincidence that just as gay people won a fighting chance to survive, the culture that grew up around us and gave us a unique means of expression and a sense of identity disappeared into the morass of the mainstream.

"We come across some noble grief," Wilde wrote, "that we think will lend the purple dignity of tragedy to our days, but it passes away from us, and things less noble take its place, and on some grey windy dawn, or odorous eve of silence and of silver, we find ourselves looking with callous wonder, or dull heart of stone, at the trees of gold-flecked hair that we had once so wildly worshipped and so madly kissed."

Where once there was vivid difference, and a culture that grew from and supported that difference, now we find ourselves regarding the increasingly faint symbols and signs of our difference "with callous wonder," asking ourselves what ever could have been appealing or important about those aspects of gay life that set us apart from the rest of the world—those "trees of gold-flecked hair that we had once so wildly worshipped and so madly kissed."

But it's always better to move boldly forward than to stand around gawking for long at the past. Ideally, we should know the value of what is lost, and accept that it is mostly going or gone. We want to be neither cynical (which is to know, according to Wilde, "the price of everything and the value of nothing") nor sentimental (seeing "an absurd value in everything" but not knowing "the market price of any single thing").

There was a time, I remember, when most of us had at least one friend who would take great delight in singing in a full voice along with the original cast soundtrack of *Hello, Dolly!* or *The Girl Who Came to Supper.* Most of those friends are gone now, at least mine are, and it's as if they took gay culture with them when they left us. Sometimes that full-throated singing of theirs could be terribly irritating, and it usually went on for far too long. But it stopped, for me, far too abruptly. Which is typical of life, whether within or without a gay culture. "Things last," as Oscar Wilde—our patron saint—said, "either too long, or not long enough."

<〈◇〉>

It was during the twentieth century that homosexuality in America went from being almost literally unmentionable to being an open subject that only the most rigidly conservative, roughly redneck (or closeted) types could muster the energy to disdain. Homosexuality's exposure of itself and the acceptance of it by a majority of people did not happen overnight, of course, and it did not happen of its own accord, by some natural or inevitable historical process. The gay rights movement is ultimately one of the great (and one of the few) success stories in the history of American politics.

In Daniel Harris's 1997 *The Rise and Fall of Gay Culture,* he makes the thrilling argument that the history of gay culture from the 1950s to the 1980s can be charted by watching the transformation over time of gay porn films. They started out, in the '50s, as short films about "such unspeakably obscene things as naked teenagers skinny dipping in mountain lakes, bare-assed cowboys in G-strings and Stetsons tackling unsuspecting Indian braves, and pensive artists sketching nude athletes in the tasteful poses of classical discus throwers." The stag films of the 1970s were amateurish, arty, plot-thick (and often very sexy) productions in which "we enter what might be called a dreamscape, an hypnotic and decidedly ill-lit world. . . ." These gay porn films "became more raunchy and less euphemistic" and featured, for the first time, every sort of penetration imaginable. The aim was to show real people having real sex and enjoying it, to put it politely. By the mid-1980s, porn films had gone from focusing "on what the actors were *feeling* when they had sex" to focusing "on how they *look* when they engaged in it." The new pornography, which is brightly lit and features smooth, athletic, well-hung, clean-shaven young men, Harris writes, "shows us how sex *should* look, not how it really looks." This shift in gay pornography is matched on a sociological level by the "out and proud" stance in which gay people have embraced identification as a large, relatively wealthy demographic class that is eagerly and expensively sought after by advertisers and politicians. Gay men live now, at least on TV and in the popular imagination (and in porn films), in a well-lit world populated by clean, good-looking, clean-shaven, healthy young men. This recent demographification of the homosexual male is celebrated by some and regretted by a few. In any case, it's where we are as American gays now: in full view.

Looking at gay American literature is another way of tracing the history of homosexuality in this country over the course of the twentieth century. The beginning was slow: a few novels referred somewhat obliquely to the attraction, not necessarily of a sexual nature, of one person to another who happened to be of the same sex. Most of the early literary texts with any sort of gay theme were not well-known or popular books.

In 1906, a novel called *Imre*, by Edward Irenaeus Prime-Stevenson, an American who used the pseudonym Xavier Mayne, was privately printed in Naples. It was, according to Byrne R. S. Fone in *A Road to Stonewall: Male Homosexuality and Homophobia in English and American Literature*, 1750–1969, "the first homosexual novel written by an American in which there is no dissembling, no coded discourse, no pretense that friendship is Platonic or that desire is allegorical." It was also, according to Fone, not "a very 'good' book." Even so, I have tried for years to find a copy of it for sale, but never have. It gives new meaning to the term "out of print."

Robert McAlmon was an interesting gay expatriate from Kansas living in Paris during the 1920s. His collection of stories, *Distinguished Air: Grim Fairy Tales,* was published there (in an edition of 115 copies) in 1925, reprinted in New York in 1963 as *There Was a Rustle of Black Silk Stockings,* and again in 1992 as *Miss Knight and Others* with a foreword by Gore Vidal. The best of the stories, "Miss Knight," is about a tough-talking, cocaine-snorting, promiscuous queen in Berlin. The opening lines are typical of the writing: "With her it was 'now I'm tellin' you, Mary,' or 'now when these bitches get elegant I lay 'em out stinkin',' many times a day, if her mood was a vital one. Apparently he, to the outside world of acute observation, she would hastily apologize had she used the Mary phrase on a man who did not know her well, or who might resent queerness and undue familiarity."

Another early gay novel was Robert Scully's *A Scarlet Pansy,* which was published by a small press in New York in 1933, but was probably written a decade earlier. The outrageous hero/heroine of this picaresque story is Fay Etrange, a drag queen sex addict from Kuntsville, Pennsylvania. Young Fay moves first to Baltimore and then to other big cities, bedding every sort of man that crosses her path, from soldiers to lifeguards to policemen and athletes, though before very long at all she "had become a oncer—that is, she was through with a man after one experience." Scully was a good writer, with a great knack for camp style and a wicked sense of humor. Though Fay is referred to throughout as a "she," it's perfectly obvious—and meant to be—that "she" is a gay man. As a child, Fay is forced to work in the fields of her family's farm. "She was strong and healthy. But there was that in her cheeks, her eyes, even her hair, that proclaimed her sexually different. Mentally, too, there was a hidden unrest dimly perceived by her brother Bill who showed his resentment by taunting her continually on her *ladylike* ways." Fay doesn't stick around for such torment in Kuntsville for long, though. Her first real love affair is with a cowboy who's "tall, tanned, handsome, strong and virile." He, like most of the men she meets, is instantly devoted to Fay and can't get enough of her. "Over and over when they were alone he would say, 'I wish it was possible for us to marry. God! Wouldn't that be great?'" Fay explains that it's just as well that they can't get married, since she would just have to find another lover shortly thereafter since the cowboy would surely be worn out before long. "'We'd better thank God that marriage is entirely out of the question,' 'Well, love is not,' sighed Cowboy. 'Crawl right up into my arms, honey, and love me some more.' They were off again."

The Gay Century got started, in terms of its full flowering in literature, a little late. But once it had bloomed, it thrived. The history of gay American literature in the twentieth century is glorious, filled with a spectacular variety, energy, and surprise.

NONE OF HENRY BLAKE FULLER'S (1857-1929) seven novels sold many copies, and all of them except *Bertram Cope's Year* are now long out of print, which is a gratifying irony given that it was, of all his books, the most completely ignored upon publication and the only one with a gay theme. No one, apparently, knew in 1919 what to make of a novel about a young man who rejects the advances of several ardent females and a professor in order to live quietly with an effeminate boyfriend in Wisconsin. Fuller's civilized friends, the upper crust of Chicago society, were embarrassed by his unaccustomed candor—they thought of him as a respectable, reserved bachelor and the author of serious, realistic novels mostly about the discrepancy between European sophistication and the imperfect human products of American capitalism. When Joseph A. Matter gave a talk to the Chicago Literary Club about Fuller in 1965, claiming to be something of an expert on Fuller's work, he confessed (or boasted) of never even having read *Bertram Cope's Year* since it was "dull and lacking in point or purpose." He misquoted one of the few comments about the novel published between the time of the book's appearance and his talk, an article by Burton Rascoe from the early 1920s. Rascoe had written, "It may be said that *Bertram Cope's Year*, in so far as it was read and understood at all, shocked Mr. Fuller's friends so painfully that they silenced it into limbo. It is a story, delicately done with the most exquisite taste, of a sublimated irregular affection. It received scant and unintelligent notice from the reviewers, and though it was filled with dynamite scrupulously packed, it fell harmless as a dud, only to be whispered about here and there by grave people who wondered why Mr. Fuller should choose such a theme." The publisher of the book, Ralph Seymour, told Mr. Matter, "No one seemed to want it and I'll bet I didn't sell 200 copies."

Available now in at least two editions, one with an introduction by Edmund Wilson and an afterword by Andrew Solomon, *Bertram Cope's Year* survives as an early classic, gay American novel. It is uniquely funny and it has a special kind of eroticism that's the result of the author's discreet, pointed technique of suggesting an erotic situation that could always pass, if necessary, for ordinary, innocent life in a college town.

What the book is really about is stated best by Wilson in the 1970 *New Yorker* article that has been reprinted as the introduction to the novel. The "real point of the story" is "that Bertram's admirers all look to find in him a version of a semidivine ideal that he makes no attempt to live up to; that he is quite unconscious that his beauty and charm, together with a hard, self-sufficient core of character, have caused them to endow him with qualities which he does not at all possess." Cope is far from stupid, but he is blithely oblivious to most of the amorous feelings he stirs up in just about everyone around him.

‹◊›

In a 1922 essay, Carl Van Vechten, speaking generally of Fuller's technique as a novelist, wrote, "Fuller's touch is like the lifting of an eyebrow, the quick flash of an ash from a cigarette...." Van Vechten strives for the same sort of loaded discretion and insinuation in his essay. In the one sentence that purports to state the theme of *Bertram Cope's Year* (which Van Vechten inaccurately claims to be identical to that of Thomas Mann's *Death in Venice*), he uses the mildest of words to describe a situation in Fuller's novel that could surely be spoken of in more erotic, passionate ways; and yet his use of one word (*boy*) gives the impression of a lechery and pedophilia that the book itself does not. "*Bertram Cope's Year* deals with the affection felt by a middle-aged man for a young boy, the boy's instinctive rejection of this unwelcome attention, and his acceptance of a certain more plausible affiliation." Bertram Cope is in graduate school when the novel begins—he is "about twenty-four"; the middle-aged man feels more than affection for him—he feels lust, and possibly a kind of love; and the "certain more plausible affiliation" refers to Cope's lover, with whom he goes off in the end to live happily, perhaps, ever after. What's most interesting of all about Van Vechten's purported synopsis of Fuller's novel is its emphasis on the older man, Basil Randolph, a kind and harmless professor, rather than on the title character, who unlike Randolph appears in nearly every scene of the book. When Van Vechten wrote his essay he was himself a married man in his early forties who had had his share of flirtations with younger men.

The theme of a younger man decisively spurning an older one, letting the chips fall where they will, suggests two tragic possibilities: that of the younger man's gradual discovery that love is hard to come by and should never have been casually cast away, even when it came from an unexciting source; and the more obvious—and more poignant—tragedy of the older man's lonely middle years giving way gradually to an equally lonely old age. The older man has the advantage of knowing what's coming, and he can prepare himself for it by surrounding himself with friends, looking for more responsive objects for his affection, and not expecting anything much from young men (though he may well be more or less helpless in his passion). But these advantages, of course, only add to the pathos of the old man's folly. Bertram Cope, on the other hand, who is pursued throughout the novel by a variety of characters, male and female—that is, in fact, about all that happens in this very dry though strangely compelling and amusing novel—has no idea that his popularity, which baffles him in the first place, will fade along with his youth. It never occurs to Bertram, and is never stated by anyone else (though it is certainly implied by the author), that a good deal of Bertram's "charm" is the direct result of his ostensible availability combined with his youthful good looks, which are his (as they are anyone's) only for a few short years. As a friend of mine likes to say, we're old for a lot longer than we're young.

What does not happen in the novel, but often does in real life, is that yet another, handsomer, smarter young man comes along and settles the matter for a while by sweeping our hero off his mystified feet, thus causing yet another tragedy—that of the hero's frumpy boyfriend, who in the novel is nervously waiting in the wings to be abandoned and embittered.

‹◊›

In the novel's first chapter, "Cope at a College Tea," Bertram meets the formidable widow Medora T. Phillips, who will be the oldest (and most brazen) of his fervent admirers. He speaks with her for the first time while she firmly holds his hand, "returning her unabashed pressure with a hearty good will and blazing down upon her through his clear blue eyes with a high degree of self-possession, even of insouciance." She is instantly addicted. Cope languidly explains, "with a liberal exhibition of perfect teeth," that he'd been teaching literature for two years in Wisconsin but had come back to school for an

advanced degree, which for Mrs. Phillips apparently represents the height of romantic questing and valor.

When Cope first meets Basil Randolph at the same tea party, Randolph too is quite floored by the young man's exemplary (though far from extravagant) good manners. He ruminates longingly about Cope's simple kindness: ". . . he had shown himself so damnably tender toward a man fairly advanced within the shadow of the fifties. . . ." The novel is a tour-de-force comic playing-out of the various characters' passions for Cope and his attempts to avoid getting involved with anyone but Arthur Lemoyne, the "plump" young man with "liquid," dark eyes whom he prefers over all the others.

Arthur eventually joins Bertram in Churchton, the college town (based on Evanston, Illinois) in which the novel is set. Arthur's passion, apart from Bertram, is for theater, and he is cast in the current college production—as a woman, a role he plays all too well. The night before the first dress rehearsal of the play, Bertram's roommate and lover, according to the interested and opionated narrator, "was a good deal occupied with wigs and lingerie. Here one detail leads to another, and anyone who goes in wholeheartedly may go in dreadfully deep. Their room came to be strown with all the disconcerting items of a theatrical wardrobe. Cope soon reached the point where he was not quite sure that he liked it all, and he began to develop a distaste for Lemoyne's preoccupation with it. He came home one afternoon to find on the corner of his desk a long pair of silk stockings and a too dainty pair of ladies' shoes. 'Oh, Art!' he protested." But Bertram enjoys the performance a few days later, though it is too much for the likes of Mrs. Phillips. Arthur, whose complexion, like his eyes, is on the dark side, wore a wig that "was of a sunny blond hue. Its curls, as palpably artificial as they were voluminous, made his eyes look darker and somehow more liquid than ever. The contrast was piquant, almost sensational." No one enjoys the performance more than Arthur himself, who has a real knack for drag, both onstage and off. But after the show, backstage, in a fatal moment of postperformance recklessness, Arthur, still dressed up, makes a pass at a straight boy.

> He continued to act off-stage; and in his general state of ebulliency he endeavored to bestow a measure of upwelling femininity upon another performer who was in the dress of his own sex. This downright fellow, in a cutaway and silk hat, did not understand,—or at least had no patience with a role carried too far. He brusquely cleared himself of Lemoyne's arm with a good vigorous push. This effort not only propelled Lemoyne against some scenery and left him, despite the voluminous blond wig, with a bruise on his forehead; it immediately pushed him out of his part, and it ended by pushing him out of the organization and even out of the University.
>
> "Keep off, will you!" said the young *elegant* crudely.
>
> Lemoyne's "atmosphere" dissipated suddenly. His art-structure collapsed.

This is an embarrassing episode for the quiet and well-mannered, studious Bertram, but, after finishing his degree, he goes back to Wisconsin to be with his exiled lover before they head East, where Bertram is to take up a post at "an important university."

‹◊›

The novel ends with no suicides or rending of garments or hopelessness. Despite the dramatic "collapse" of poor Arthur's "art-structure," once he and Bertram have gone, life in Churchton, it is implied, will go on much as before. Basil Randolph swears that next year he will not "'cultivate' some other young chap," but will concentrate more on his work and his old friends. He and Mrs. Phillips have become closer than they were when the novel began, and they intend to rely on each other more in the future. Bertram Cope will fade from memory, which, along with growing older, is what young men do, according to the novel's wistful theme. Basil Randolph, thinking about Cope as he does so often, says to a friend in a rare moment of clearheadedness: "Why does anybody care? And for what? For the thing that is just out of reach. He's cool; he's selfish; he's indifferent. Yet, somehow, frost and fire join end to end and make the circle complete."

The circle completed by frost and fire—youth's cool indifference and maturity's frustrated, burning desire—is as old as the concept of passionate love itself. Bertram Cope's year of unwanted and undeserved attention is a paradigm for youth, and his story is a kind of melancholy myth about wasted affection and the primacy of everyday, domestic love, as well as a comedy of manners that shows the foolishness of the idle and the pretentious. Love, for Fuller, is not a commodity that can be bought or arranged—it's the healthy connection that sometimes persists between two people despite the connivings and the desperation of others. That this sturdy connection was described as the bond between two men in 1919, in a beautifully understated and relatively unknown novel, is one of the lovely minor miracles of American literature.

SHORTLY AFTERWARD, during the 1920s, a literary cult sprang up in both London and New York that was devoted to a very different spirit from that of the reserved Henry Blake Fuller; this cult was devoted not to the mythology of durable and domestic love, but to the spirit of Oscar Wilde and the investigation and celebration of the frivolous. The aloof leader of this very delicate and sensitive pack was the Englishman Ronald Firbank (1886–1926), whose novels, with titles such as *The Flower Beneath the Foot* and *Concerning the Eccentricities of Cardinal Pirelli*, can still exert a strange power to transport the susceptible reader into a totally unreal, bizarre, hilarious world in which there are scenes such as this:

"Ah! How clever, Shakespeare!" the Countess was saying. "How gorgeous! How glowing! I once knew a speech from 'Julia Sees Her! . . .' perhaps his greatest *oeuvre* of all. Yes! 'Julia *Sees* Her' is what I like best of that great, great master."

The English Ambassadress plied her fan.

"Friends, Comrades, Countrymen," she murmured, "I used to know it myself!"

But the lady nibbling almonds was exciting a certain amount of comment. This was the Duchess of Varna, voted by many to be one of the handsomest women of the Court. Living in economical obscurity nearly half the year round, her appearances at the palace were becoming more and more infrequent.

"I knew the Varnas were very hard up, but I did not know they were *starving*," the Countess Yvorra, a woman with a would-be indulgent face that was something less hard than rock, remarked to her neighbour the Count of Tolga, and dropping her glance from the Count's weak chin she threw a fleeting smile towards his wife, who was looking "Eastern" swathed in the skin of a blue panther.

Firbank's dozen or so novels, taken together, stand as the most extravagantly lightsome and willfully frivolous body of work by any novelist of the twentieth century—and among the most exquisite. His texts are completely *sui generis*, original, and resistant to interpretation; they have a rare, cultivated beauty with which no one has ever even sought to compete, though Firbank has had his imitators and payers of respect and homage, several of whom were his contemporaries.

One English novelist who followed Firbank in attempting a lighter-than-air, melodramatic style with some success (though he was far from popular or well-known) was Richard Oke, whose wonderful 1929 *Frolic Wind* opens with a Miss Jewell on a terrace, observing the ladies on the lawn, including the tragicomic mistress of the estate: "The after-lunch talk was breaking up, and Lady Athaliah was already stumping away toward her tower."

Such English novelists as these and their American counterparts adored French novels and poetry, especially the work of Huysmans, Gautier, Verlaine, Baudelaire, and Mallarmé. According to Edmund Wilson in his 1923 essay "Late Violets from the Nineties," they "belong essentially to the *Yellow Book* era" during which Aubrey Beardsley and Wilde and others were making their rebellious pleas for a new morality in reaction to Victorian Christianity, of which they had grown thoroughly tired. The "Yellow Book era" (loosely speaking, the 1890s) was so named after a short-lived journal, *The Yellow*

Book, which was itself named after the color of cloth in which certain distinctly exotic and fabulous French novels were bound during the mid- to late nineteenth century. In Wilde's novel, Dorian Gray educates himself in vice partly by reading one such "poisonous book," Joris-Karl Huysmans's 1884 *A Rebours* or *Against Nature*. "It was the strangest book that he had ever read," wrote Wilde. "It seemed to him that in exquisite raiment and to the delicate sound of flutes, the sins of the world were passing in dumb show before him. Things that he had dimly dreamed of were suddenly made real to him. Things of which he had never dreamed were gradually revealed." *A Rebours* was hugely influential both in the 1890s and again in the 1920s. It is the story of Duc Jean Floressas des Esseintes, a "frail young man of thirty who was anaemic and highly strung, with hollow cheeks, cold eyes of steely blue, a nose which was turned up but straight, and thin, papery hands." Des Esseintes is the last of a long line that has become increasingly effete; he is a true dandy, the bane of whose existence is "human mediocrity." He is spiritually ill and drawn inevitably to practices, ideas, books, and art that bespeak decay, corruption, and a transfixing, lugubrious play of mystery and shadow.

In *Decadence: The Strange Life of an Epithet*, Richard Gilman writes that "themes of spiritual malaise, fatal enchantment, and seduction by the idea of corruption were precisely those that attracted a type of inexperienced Anglo-Saxon mind to the French." The writings of such authors as Huysmans and the Marquis de Sade, Theophile Gautier's *Mademoiselle de Maupin* (in which a young poet and his mistress both fall in love with a woman disguised as a boy), and much of the French poetry in the nineteenth century, offered to the English-speaking aficionados of "decadence" an example of imaginative work in which a developed, arresting predilection for the artificial, the subversive, and the marginal was taken seriously without being drained of its attractively shiny, witty, glamorous surface qualities. Another of the influences on Wilde and his peers in London, as well as the British and American writers of the '20s, was the legendary Beau Brummell, the first dandy, who himself influenced the French when he moved to Paris in 1816 with his dazzling gift for being himself (and never struggling, even slightly, to be anything else).

What all these influences on the school-of-frivolity writers of the 1920s had in common was an inclination toward mockery of the sacred and the accepted; and a high degree of tolerance for treatments of such subjects as work, social position, and sexuality that were noticeably less earnest than the literary and artistic work on the same themes in the past. In 1894, Wilde wrote in a letter that "... to the world I seem, by intention on my part, a dilettante and dandy merely—it is not wise to show one's heart to the world—and as seriousness of manner is the disguise of the fool, folly in its exquisite modes of triviality and indifference and lack of care is the role of the wise man."

The crucial difference between the writers of the 1890s and those of the 1920s is that the later writers lived in a time and a place in which Victorian Christianity had already become, at least in certain sophisticated circles, completely outdated and thoroughly, at times even mockingly, dismissed. These later writers, according to Wilson, are "able to take their heresies and pleasures lightly.... But it is probably no longer possible for practitioners of this species of fantasy to become either worried or fervent. The generation of Beardsley and Wilde had been brought up on Ruskin and Tennyson; but the generation of Firbank and Van Vechten has been brought up on Beardsley and Wilde, and their prejudices were undermined early.

The First Time I Met Frank O'Hara

The conviction of sin has been removed, and it is possible for the 'sinner' to be amiable again. This fin de siecle genre may be destined to grow dimmer and dimmer, but at least it fades away with a smile."

‹◊›

By the early 1920s, in New York City, "sin" was already definitely passé, and paganism was all the rage—the wild ones were no longer necessarily social outcasts; many of them were popular and closely read, watched, and followed. By the time Carl Van Vechten (1880–1964) published *The Blind Bow-Boy* in 1923 (at Knopf, among the most prestigious literary book publishers in the United States), his homosexual characters and jokes were not only admissible, they were fashionable. While his male characters were not described as hanging around in gay bars or explicitly having sex with other men, many of them were clearly gay or bisexual, as Van Vechten himself was (though he was married to Fania Marinoff, an actress). And if not gay themselves, almost all of his characters were at least gay friendly and worldly wise.

Had Van Vechten had a more lasting and widespread success (which is to say, had he been more powerfully original as a novelist than he was), Campaspe Lorillard, his most fabulous character in *The Blind Bow-Boy*, might have become a lasting national symbol for 1920s New York amorality. She was, according to Wilson, Van Vechten's "most successful achievement." She is the perfect friend to gay men, married to a rich, unattractive businessman who longs to spend time with her, but who accepts her outlandish demands for fear of losing her permanently. Campaspe is a woman who likes to be left alone until she feels inclined to have company—and then the company must be very amusing, preferably good-looking, and not too earnest. She has a philosophy of nonchalance that she spins out at length and with pleasure (she does nothing if it's not a pleasure). After hearing of a friend, Amy, having lost her privilege to use Gramercy Park for smoking within the sacrosanct gates of New York's most visible private space (then and now), Campaspe diagnoses Amy's problems:

> She doesn't understand how to enjoy her freedom. She doesn't understand her world. She wants to live her own life, as she sees us live ours, and she doesn't know how. She's always having keys taken away from her. Everything will be locked to her soon.
>
> ... Amy is trying too hard to fight the world, to soften the world's corners, instead of softening her own. In the end, of course, martyrdom is waiting for her. I have no respect for martyrs. Any one who is strong enough shapes the world to his own purposes, but he doesn't do it roughly; he accomplishes his object in just the way that any woman you know gets anything she wants out of her husband ... by appearing to be in sympathy with those who oppose him. Conform externally with the world's demands and you will get anything you desire in life. By a process of erosion you can dig a hole in two years through public opinion that it would take you two centuries to knock through. It is just as great a mistake to reject violently ideas that do not appeal to us. Rejection implies labour, interest, even fear. Indifference is the purer method. Indifference rids one of cause and effect simultaneously. . . . The world—she appeared to be in a kind of revery—is a very pleasant place for people who know how to live. We are the few.

The Blind Bow-Boy (the title refers to Cupid, a fountain statue of whom is in Campaspe's garden; she also mockingly calls her husband

Cupid) is the story of Harold Prewett, an eager and innocent young man who grew up "among the flutter of petticoats" with his Aunt Sadi, "a large woman, with large bones, large hands, large feet, a large nose, and large eyes. She had a large mole on her throat under her large left ear." It's pretty clear that Aunt Sadi was a lesbian: she was not married, had only a few friends, "and those few were all women." Among the books to be found in Aunt Sadi's house are a novel called *Nothing to Wear* and Melville's *Redburn*. Harold grows up a sensitive and isolated boy without the influence of any paternal figure, "too well-dressed for his environment," in Sadi's Connecticut farmhouse.

> In his senior year [of high school] he had achieved a slender
> philosophy. He accepted, in his modest fashion, the fact that
> there were unknown sins in the world. He even became a trifle
> cynical in an humble and apologetic way: he seemed to be so
> separated from others by his temperament and breeding. More
> and more he was alone.

When the novel opens, Harold has recently graduated from college; he is still awkward and unsure of himself as he waits, in a parlor, to see his father for the first time. His father, a rich businessman, surprises Harold by offering to set him up in a townhouse near Gramercy Park with a butler and plenty of money, the only proviso being that Harold *not* go into business, particularly not "the cloak and suit business," which is the father's line of work. "You must see more of life and learn to live," his father says to Harold. He has decided to conduct an experiment, hiring for Harold a "tutor" whose qualifications were that he should have "no moral sense," that he should

know three languages and possess a sense of humor, that he should have been "the central figure in some public scandal," and is younger than thirty.

The man Mr. Prewett hires, Paul Moody, fits the bill exactly. He is a dandy with a busy social life and no material aspirations apart from, perhaps, eventually marrying a rich woman.

The butler hired to look after young Harold, an experienced man called Oliver Drains, tells Harold of his previous employer, the Duke of Middlebottom. When Harold asks why he left the Duke, Drains explains: "One of his young ladies wished to whip me, sir. The incident aroused the Duke. He forgot himself, sir."

Harold, himself quite scandalized by all these events, makes an unconscious plea for normalcy by "falling in love" with Alice Blake, a pretty, dull girl he meets when the taxi she's in is rammed by a truck, leaving her unharmed but concerned that the driver of the cab she was in not be blamed for the accident. She and Harold (who witnessed the accident) appear in court in the cabdriver's defense, and so begins an affair that results eventually in their marriage, which lasts only a short time.

All of this, though the central story line, is peripheral to the main action of the novel, which is largely taken up with describing the fast-paced urban life of Paul Moody (the "tutor"), Campaspe Lorillard (his best friend), and their circle of pleasure-seeking urban companions. During an outing to Coney Island, they meet the sixteen-year-old Zimbule, a snake charmer in the sideshow. Campaspe interviews the girl about her work and her life. Why, she wants to know, did Zimbule agree to work with such frightening animals?

> Coin. You gotta eat.
> Hungry?
> Ain't had a good feed for a week.
> Where do you live?
> No place.
> Where's your family?
> In hell, I guess.
> Any friends?
> Don't kid me.

Campaspe and her entourage whisk the dazzling girl away and off to Manhattan, where she easily seduces everyone she meets and joins the cast of characters. Had the story been set fifty years later, they would have gone directly to Studio 54.

Another addition to the group is none other than the Duke of Middlebottom, Drains' previous employer, a grand queen with a stutter who always has his hotel rooms re-wallpapered in Japanese prints that are "erotic and often obscene," and whose motto, printed on his stationery, is "A thing of beauty is a boy for ever." Harold is immediately impressed by the Duke's "grace and charm," and the Duke "manifested an interest in Harold which appeared to be sincere." The Duke "questioned Harold regarding his tastes, and told him long stories of harmless adventures among the Italian peasantry, in which shepherd boys and bersaglieri figured in sympathetic guises." The Duke takes a furnished townhouse on West Twelfth Street and proposes that the group produce a light summer opera there. Ideas for the play are tossed out and rejected, among them a setting of Ronald Firbank's *The Princess Zoubaroff*. Finally they decide on "L'Après-midi Byzantine," an obscure play "in one act and no costumes: cool for the actors, and hot for the spectators." Everyone takes either a role in the play or offstage managing the show. Zimbule, naturally, is the star as "the boy" to the Duke's "charioteer." When it comes time to find an audience, Campaspe suggests that the Duke invite his friends. "I have no f-f-f-friends, retorted the Duke, only people that amuse me, and people I sleep with. . . . The people that amuse me are all in the p-p-p-play. . . . The theatre isn't b-b-b-b-b-big enough to hold the others." Somehow, though, the Duke finds an appropriately glamorous audience, "a splendid, showy throng," and the play is a success, with Zimbule's performance as the boy particularly "rich and strange."

The First Time I Met Frank O'Hara

The next day begins for Campaspe, not unusually, at one o'clock in the afternoon, when she reads letters from her two sons, Basil and Esmé, who are spending the summer with their grandfather in the country.

Esmé had caught a blue-fish and Basil wanted a cowboy's suit with chaps, a red-flannel shirt, a sombrero, and a lariat. Both of them desired to see their mother. Wasn't she coming down? She tapped an envelope against her open lips as she thought of her sons. Campaspe loved her children, and occasionally she had them with her. It was constitutional of her, however, to believe that she was only doing her best for others when she entirely pleased herself. . . . Boys, she felt, developed more rapidly and more individually if they did not live too much with their parents.

Next Campaspe reads a letter from Laura, a friend spending the summer in the country; she begs Campaspe to join her there. "All the world, it would seem, was calling for Campaspe, but this was invariably true, she realized, when one was enjoying oneself. It was only when one felt lonely and bored that nobody asked one to do anything or to go anywhere." This chapter of Van Vechten's novel, devoted mainly to Campaspe, is among the great scenes in gay writing before the Second World War: purely the product of a gay sensibility, in which sexuality is kept firmly beneath the surface, and the surface shines with style and wit. Campaspe expostulates upon aesthetics in literature: "Growth of character in a novel is nonsense. People never change. Psychology: the supreme imbecility." She is ideally jaded; she is worldly sophistication personified. When her husband offers to break an engagement in order to dine with her, she wonders to herself with deadpan chic, "Why was everyone so pathetic today?"

Harold (our hero) and Alice (the girl who, it turns out, is Campaspe's sister) honeymoon in Provincetown, in a cabin eccentrically decorated (but never used) by Campaspe. Their relationship becomes more and more strained due to Alice's prudishness and Harold's nostalgia for the amusing times he had among Campaspe, Paul, Zimbule, and the Duke. He escapes, in due course, and enjoys an affair with Zimbule, the nymphomaniacal snake charmer, now a famous actress.

In the end, Campaspe, in an attempt to soothe her nerves, takes a Christmas cruise alone, away from Cupid and her children and the taxing itinerary of social occasions in New York. On the deck, wrapped in a fur coat, she feels too languid even to pick up one of the books she brought along. "She had no desire, she found, to read at all. Then, immediately, she regretted that she had brought no book by Huysmans, Huysmans who had said: There are two ways of ridding ourselves of a thing which burdens us, casting it away or letting it fall. To cast away requires an effort of which we may not be capable, to let fall imposes no labour, is simpler, within the reach of all. To cast away, again, implies a certain interest, a certain animation, even a certain fear; to let fall is absolute indifference, absolute contempt...." Then she falls asleep for a while. When she wakes, with "the great disk of the fiery sun...sinking into the cold sea," she gradually becomes aware of two men standing together looking out on the water. They turn and face each other: are they in love with each other? Who are they? It's young Harold—and the Duke of Middlebottom.

‹◊›

Carl Van Vechten gave up writing fiction in 1930 when *Parties*, his seventh novel, was poorly reviewed and failed to sell well. He took up, instead, photographing his famous friends and the attractive men he met. There are still men in New York who claim to have been photographed nude by Carl Van Vechten in his palatial apartment on Central Park West. His most popular novel, *The Tattooed Countess*, which was turned into a bad movie, is still sometimes in print along with one or two of the other novels. A biography by Bruce Kellner appeared in 1968, a selection of Van Vechten's letters, edited by Kellner, was published in 1987, and letters between Van Vechten and Langston Hughes (edited by Emily Bernard) came out in 2001. While he may or may not have been a "great writer"—he is not much remembered these days as a novelist—there are aspects of his work that speak more touchingly and more directly to at least one *type* of gay experience in the United States than, perhaps, any other American author. The type is of the precocious, sensitive boy who longs to achieve his full realization and happiness in a large, exciting city far from his humble home. Gareth Johns, the hero of *The Tattooed Countess*, a seventeen-year-old very much like Van Vechten himself, speaks of a wish that is a kind of gay American refrain, which has, perhaps, a resonance for all sorts of people trapped in small places who wish for more from life than they're getting:

> I want to know everything, *everything* . . . and . . . I'm going to. . . . I want to get away from this town. . . . I want to visit the theatre and the opera and the art galleries. I want to meet people. I want to learn. Somewhere there must be more people like me. . . .

There were, of course, people like him, and Van Vechten wasted little time in finding them. Shortly after moving to New York, he began to circle continuously and enthusiastically around the center of modern cultural life there—he loved classical music, ballet, "Negro culture" and Harlem, jazz, movies; and he knew many of the best writers of his time, including Gertrude Stein, Wallace Stevens, and the young James Purdy. He was born in 1880 in Cedar Rapids, Iowa, the last child of a fairly wealthy family. His father was a liberal, thoughtful man who helped found a school for black children in Mississippi. Van Vechten was exposed early and often to the best cultural events, ideas, and books within reach; after receiving a degree from the University of Chicago in 1903, he moved to New York, where he was a music critic for the *New York Times* and later the city's first serious ballet critic. In 1926, he published *Nigger Heaven*, a controversial novel he published under that title against the wishes of most of his friends and his own dying father. He also persuaded his friend Ronald Firbank to change the title of a novel published in England as *Sorrow in Sunlight* to *Prancing Nigger* for the American edition. In a clumsy effort to defuse that derogatory bomb of a word, he mostly succeeded only in appearing insensitive at best and a condescending fool at worst.

But Van Vechten did present to the world, in his life and in his work, a type of gay man that he was unashamed of being—sophisticated, uncloseted (*and* married), intelligent, enthusiastic. His sexuality was among the undercurrents in his psyche, as it were, rather than a definition of him—he was, like Thoreau and Whitman, a "natural man," but in a very "unnatural" context. He hated to be in the country and lived in Manhattan all his life, traveling occasionally only to other cities. He stands now as a model of the man-about-town who does what interests him, keeps company with whom he likes, and declares no purpose apart from the dissemination and creation of beauty in all of its artificial manifestations.

Aspects of his personality can still be found in some urban gay men, mostly of a certain age—but those traces that linger get paler and rarer all the time, and they often go unappreciated and even unnoticed. I celebrate them here and pay them some modest homage. To the remaining dandies in the world—to those who live each day, every day, for beauty and art—I say (quoting the epigraph, by Raymond Radiguet, to Van Vechten's last novel), *Ce n'est pas dans la nouveauté, c'est dans l'habitude que nous trouvons les plus grands plaisirs.* It is not in the new, but in everyday experience that we find our greatest pleasure.

VAN VECHTEN'S CLOSE FRIEND Gertrude Stein (1874-1946) was famous, she believed, not for the books she wrote that people were able to understand, but for the obscure works that leave most people at least a little baffled and feeling amused, impressed, or bamboozled. Had she written only *Three Lives*, *The Autobiography of Alice B. Toklas*, *Everybody's Autobiography*, and *Wars I Have Seen*, she would have proven herself to be a fascinating if somewhat pretentious writer, but not the Modernist oracle and the singer of strange lesbian songs that readers have puzzled passionately over for nearly a hundred years now—not, that is, the genius she believed herself unquestionably to have been.

Stein was a rebellious, unconventional woman from the beginning. According to Brenda Wineapple's 1996 *Sister Brother: Gertrude & Leo Stein*, "If [Gertrude] generally looked the part of the typical Radcliffe undergraduate . . . she also wore a battered sailor hat, remembered a former schoolmate, 'until it became so disreputable that a friend placed it deep in an ash barrel.'" One of the forces behind Stein's lifelong literary project was surely her sense that she was different, in a radical way, from most people, and she certainly sought to create a body of work very much unlike anyone else's. Her writings, taken together, can be seen as a kind of battle between received language (the way most people use language most of the time in everyday life) and linguistic invention or experimentation. Critic Richard Poirier, in *Trying It Out in America: Literary and Other Performances* writes, "A reader who wants to enter into the movements of Stein's language had best read her without caring too strictly about any of her various schematizations of private as against public writing. It is better to think of each piece, particularly when it is experimental to one degree or another, as constituting a scene in the dramatization of her degrees of estrangement from normative English. There is scarcely any work of hers, including the more conventional ones, that isn't to some extent an act of linguistic protest against traditional and agreed-upon systems of designation and against the structures of relative primacy and subordination that have been made to seem necessary, normal, and inevitable."

Yes, but what are we to make of a novel such as Stein's 1930 *Lucy Church Amiably* that *begins* with this maddening though melliflu-ous utterance: "There were as many chairs there and there were two a chair that can be found everywhere a rocking chair that is to say a rocking chair can be found everywhere." A friend of mine, who was unfamiliar with Stein's work, listening to me read aloud from this novel, remarked that it sounded to her like Dr. Seuss, which she did not mean as a criticism. Just as we all have memories from childhood of language that lulled and consoled, so, on reading Stein's crazy, rhyming prose, we can enjoy the pleasing musical effect, almost like that of listening to a song in a language we don't know. There's a deep melody, a rhythm, and a form. Names and other words get repeated like musical themes. Reading a long series of such sentences encour-ages us to read very differently from usual, with less expectation and more concern for a lyrical quality than we typically get from prose lit-erature. The reader of an experimental Stein novel such as *Lucy Church Amiably* or the much longer *The Making of Americans* needn't feel any need to read straight through from the beginning to the end (just try it!). There are no rules to reading a Stein text, though it may prove helpful to relax a little, to accept what is given, to try to enjoy the experience Stein created just as it is. There's nothing confusing about *Lucy Church Amiably*—appreciating it is like appreciating nature: though it will be utterly unchanged by our appreciation, we may find ourselves, surprisingly, subtly changed by it.

‹◊›

"Pink Melon Joy," written during the First World War and published in the 1922 collection *Geography and Plays*, is one of Stein's wildly experimental texts that has come to be understood as distinctly lesbian. When Stein wrote it, she had recently fallen in love with Alice Toklas, and they had begun sleeping together every night (or rather every morning, since Stein was in the habit of staying up very late to work in silence). The writing here is cute and fun, and sometimes gorgeous, as in this section with the heading "I do not."

> Their thoughts were of one another.
> The maid a very pretty girl somewhat showily dressed in a costume composed of the royal colors fixed curious eyes down a long passage and a short one. Presently the girl in blue returned.
> Blue and white.
> Returned.
> Food and wine.
> How could it be how could it be.
> Blue and white, not an especial pinching.
> I wish I was may be I am.

Stein was one of the gay writers in the first half of the twentieth century whose style seems to be directly tied to the *suppression* of an overt description of her sexuality in print. American writers from Halleck to the young Gore Vidal (including Stein, though she spent most of her adult life in France) lived within the ethos of an American Puritan culture in which any tradition (from Greek antiquity, say, or early Asia) of writing about homosexual experience was obscured by convenient misreadings or ignorance of it. There was more openness about gay sexuality in ancient philosophy or Classical Chinese poetry than in the literary work of any American, with a few important exceptions, until after the Second World War. But far from blocking these earlier gay writers from themselves, their reluctance to write openly about their homosexuality was among their tools in fashioning an original style. Gertrude Stein would never have written such lines as "Trembling was all living, living was all loving, some one was then the other one" (from "Ada," a portrait of Alice Toklas) had she felt "free" to write more openly—and thus, perhaps, less imaginatively—about the sexual nature of her attraction to the woman in the story. And her discovery of a style of her own, likewise, must have enabled her, in some sense, to explore feelings and ideas within herself of which she might otherwise never have been made conscious. As Adam Phillips writes in *Equals*, "Good writing, like good conversation or interpretation in analysis, seems to free something in us. It is as though mobility has sprung from paralysis; but only once we start moving do we realise quite how stuck in we had been." It was at least partly *because of* her disinclination to give away too much about herself and her lover, and their private life together, that Stein was so inventive; and her inventiveness as a writer set her free to find expression for what she found within herself. Stein's whole career as a writer was devoted to describing people and things and feelings while at the same time keeping them partly hidden from view. One of the great Modernist ideals was to honor the complexity of the artist's subject, and Stein, as rigorously as any artist, acknowledged and explored the depth and the chaos—and the pleasure—of her sexuality.

Her disinclination to treat homosexuality openly and overtly, however, didn't prevent her from sneaking it into her work. In "Miss Furr and Miss Skeene," Stein portrays two "ladies" in a five-page story that uses the words *gay* or *gayer* 139 times—this in a piece that was first published in the July 1923 *Vanity Fair*. The most obvious joke of the piece is the double meaning of its favorite word, which in 1923 still meant cheerful, but had begun its transition into referring to homosexuals, depending on the context. For most readers of *Vanity Fair*, it probably just meant the former; but for the up-to-date cognoscenti and homosexuals (and Gertrude Stein was nothing if not up-to-date), it already meant both. According to historian George Chauncey, "...it was the fairies (the especially flamboyant gay men)...who used the word [*gay*] most in the 1920s and 1930s." And John Boswell, in *Christianity, Social Tolerance, and Homosexuality*, traces the word *gay* back to the Provençal word *gai*, which "was used in the thirteenth and fourteenth centuries...as a designation for the 'art of poesy' ('gai saber'), for a 'lover' ('gaiol'), and for an openly homosexual person." For us, for whom *gay* now only occasionally—and a little forcefully—can be made to take back its old meaning, the little story is hilarious, beginning with Helen Furr's outrageous name.

A young woman with "quite a pleasant home," Helen leaves her parents and travels to "a place where some were cultivating something, voices and other things needing cultivating," and there she meets Georgine Skeene, who "was cultivating her voice which some thought was quite a pleasant one." Right away, "Helen Furr and

Georgine Skeene lived together then." Miss Skeene liked to travel;
Miss Furr preferred to stay at home with Miss Skeene—"she liked to
stay in one place and be gay there." So they "travelled to another
place and stayed there and were gay there." In this place, too, everyone was cultivating something, and the women were happy. Helen
was "gay there, she was gayer and gayer there and really she was just
gay there, she was gayer and gayer there, that is to say she found ways
of being gay there that she was using in being gay there." Both of

them were "regularly gay there where they were gay. They were very regularly gay." They cultivate their voices—some said Miss Skeene's was "a better one"—and they go back to Miss Furr's pleasant home.

They settle down for a while in a place where there "were some dark and heavy men" with whom the two ladies liked to sit and talk. Georgine goes to visit her brother, and Helen stays alone "where they had been regularly living the two of them and she would then certainly not be lonesome, she would go on being gay." Eventually the women split up, and they both move away. What happens to Georgine Skeene is a mystery. But Helen Furr "was living somewhere else then and telling some about being gay and she was gay then and she was living quite regularly then. She was regularly gay then. . . . She remembered all the little ways of being gay. She was quite regularly gay. She told many then the way of being gay. She was quite regularly gay. She told many then the way of being gay, she taught very many then little ways they could use in being gay. She was living very well, she was gay then, she went on living then, she was regular in being gay, she always was living very well and was gay very well and was telling about little ways one could be learning to use in being gay, and later was telling them quite often, telling them again and again."

Gay writing has seldom been as unsentimental as this; and it has never been more lighthearted. The "moral" of this little story, which seems to have something to do with keeping cheerful and gay come what may, is brilliantly unemphatic, just casually and gingerly tossed onto the surface of the amusing, inimitable sentences. The pleasure of the text, as in all the best of Stein's linguistic compositions, is part of the text's meaning—we'll never understand it without enjoying it.

ONE IMPORTANT EXCEPTION to the rule that Americans demurred from writing openly about gay sexuality before the Second World War was *The Young and Evil*, a scandalously unembarrassed and raunchy novel of gay life in Greenwich Village by Charles Henri Ford and Parker Tyler published in Paris (and banned in the U.S.) in 1933, the same year as Stein's *Autobiography of Alice B. Toklas*. Stein said of the book when it was published that it "creates this generation as *This Side of Paradise* by Fitzgerald created his generation." Ford, who was a friend of Stein's and the lover of the Russian painter Pavel Tchelitchev, died aged ninety-four on September 27, 2002. Until then he was living on West 72nd Street, in Manhattan, where he continued to work, most recently on a series of Matisse- and surrealism-inspired paper collages that include cut-out images of hunky young men with evil erections. His selected poems, *Out of the Labyrinth*, appeared in 1991, and a volume of his diaries was published in 2001 as *Water from a Bucket: A Diary* 1948–1957 (a characteristic entry, from August 1949: "Genet thinks he can force a legend from literature—as one forces a door. But is glory stolen or conferred?")

I've been drawn to older men (some of them much older) since my teens. Ford, in his nineties, was even older than most of my "senior" friends, and once I knew he was still alive, during the summer of 2002, naturally I had to meet him. As it turned out, I met him just weeks before he died. He lived in a penthouse apartment in the Dakota, the grandest of New York buildings on Central Park West, where he lived one floor above his sister, the actress Ruth Ford. He

was well taken care of by a young man from Nepal, who was there with his two daughters when I arrived. The apartment was not grand. It was rather gloomy, in fact, and cluttered, but it did give the impression that the person who lived there was *interesting*. I had to shout to make myself heard, and Ford tended to repeat himself and was not particularly forthcoming. He did perk up a bit when I gave him a copy of my first book, a memoir of hustling, and he was happy enough to answer my questions. He told me that while *he* actually wrote *The*

The First Time I Met Frank O'Hara

Young and Evil, much of the *roman à clef* was based on shared experiences with and letters from his friend Parker Tyler (who was a fascinating writer and critic himself—he and his writings about movies are among the obsessions of Gore Vidal's title character Myra Breckinridge).

Charles Ford was determined to be famous from an early age. He told me that he was expelled from a prep school (all boys) for cutting classes, smoking in his room, and organizing "petting parties." His nickname at the time was "Hot." When he was seventeen and still living in Mississippi, he wrote in his diary lines that could have come from the teenage diaries of Andy Warhol: "In two years I will be famous. In two years I will be famous. In two years I will be famous. In two years I will be famous. In two years I will be famous. In two years I will be famous. This is my oath." Ford was not famous by the time he was nineteen, but he did find himself in contact with some famous writers, including Ezra Pound, Gertrude Stein, William Carlos Williams, and Paul Bowles, all of whom contributed to the little magazine, *Blues: A Magazine of New Rhythms*, that Ford started when he dropped out of high school in Columbus, Mississippi. (He later edited the influential and well-known surrealist journal *View*.) Parker Tyler also contributed to *Blues* and became its associate editor before ever meeting Ford; his letters to Ford persuaded the younger man that he should join Tyler in New York, which he did in 1930. "As Henry Miller said about Paris," Ford told me, "I went to New York to study vice." The life he and Tyler lived in the next year and a half in and around Greenwich Village—and the letters Tyler wrote to him after Ford sailed for Paris in May 1931—were the basis for the novel. Ford, in Paris, somewhat late according to his own schedule in the achievement of fame, wasted no time writing and publishing *The Young and Evil*, his first book, which was finished by the time he was twenty-five. In time for the publication, Charles changed his middle name, Henry, to Henri because, he says, it sounded sexier.

The Young and Evil was a book meant to command attention. The words *fairy prince* and *Lesbian* appear in the opening paragraph, and by the end of the page it's clear they're actually not "mythological creatures," but real people living openly gay lives. On that same first page, a "little girl" approaches and wonders why Karel, one of the two lead male characters (the one based on Parker Tyler), doesn't "dress in girls' clothes." She and the lesbian almost mistake him for "a Lesbian in drag," and then "for two long hours they insisted that he would do better for himself as a girl." Karel passes out; when he wakes up he finds "a nice fat old bullfrog [gay slang of the period, according to Ford, for an unattractive but harmless older man] beckoning to him." The older man offers Karel a cup of tea, and in exchange Karel, eager to exhibit his talent for poetry, recites "an old nursery rhyme he learned as a child." None of this may strike us now as particularly menacing, but the stylish writing about lesbians and bullfrogs and queer poets must have been an impressive way to open a novel in 1933.

As Steven Watson points out in his introduction to a reprint edition of the novel in 1988, "we bring to its pages the sensibility of a post-Beat, post-hippie, post-punk, post-gay liberation era. To see the novel more distinctly, we must divest ourselves of such excess consciousness, for this book belongs to an early period before the battles of the modern age had been waged." In fact, *The Young and Evil* gives an engaging portrayal of talented, sophisticated, interesting young people not all that unlike some people I know to this day. If anything, the young peo-

ple I know now are *less* apt to say things as striking (and campy) as
"[Karel's] overcoat seemed to fit him desperately," or "Julian had
shorter hair and lush expectancy," as the narrator does in introducing
the main characters early in Chapter Two. I don't wish that my friends
spoke like that, but I do feel a little regret that such signs of the difference between gay young men and straight ones are disappearing.
Assimilation entails, among other things, a less stylized use of language, which is as true of southern blacks fitting in with northern
whites as it is true of gays becoming indistinguishable from straights.
The Young and Evil is a fabulous picture of a time when fags were
glad to be queens, and part of the fun of being gay, at least for some, was
being constitutionally and happily different from other people.

The main characters of *The Young and Evil*, Julian and Karel
(based on Ford and Tyler), are wags; they're witty, smart-alecky,
adventurous urbanites. The only thing Julian has against life, he says,
is that eventually it spoils young men's mouths. The two poets, sometimes roommates, drift around New York, barely able to pay for their
drinks. They eat hot dogs for breakfast. For a cheap dinner, they go to
Fourteenth Street, "which at five o'clock is a most vulgar street,
invariably alive with the sex-starved," and have a pineapple delight.
Then they go shopping: "Karel needed an eyebrow pencil which he
bought at another counter from a salesgirl who looked mixed up" to
be selling him makeup. They try halfheartedly to help a friend raise
fifty dollars so that his girlfriend can get an abortion, and later Julian
has an affair with the father of the unwanted child, Gabriel, but not
before he and Karel both sleep with Gabriel's friend Louis. Karel ends
up in a kind of relationship with Louis; at one point he is "filled with a
sense of power because of the willingness, even eagerness, of Louis to
make their relation not a one-way affair sexually." Karel moves

uptown to be in a neighborhood where his mischievous new boyfriend Louis will, he hopes, stay away from the gangsters and the police.

When Julian (Ford) says goodbye to his roommate Karel (Tyler), about halfway through the book, he takes a moment to think about the nature of love. His thoughts ring familiar to me, nearly seventy years after they first appeared in print, and probably, I think, to most urban gay men recalling the decade of their twenties. "He had never known physical and mental love towards a single person. It had always been completely one or the other. With Karel it was the other. With Louis really neither. He was unbelieving when he saw lovers who were lovers in the complete sense and who slept night after night in the same bed. He was quite sure their love was a fabrication or a convenience or a recompense and he did not believe in their love as love."

The young and evil characters of this experimental, edgy novel are jaded: they're dulled and worn out by so much running around looking for love in all the wrong places, trying to be poets and artists and a part of the avant-garde, and asserting their right to be fully themselves, all at the same time. In a comment for the jacket of the first edition, the lesbian writer Djuna Barnes, who was a friend of Ford's, spoke of the characters' *loss* (not their rejection) of Victorian manners, customs, taste, dignity, and *victories*. The only victories these nearly exhausted characters strive for, aside from their vague dreams of artistic glory, are negative victories: not to be arrested, not to be murdered, not to be spiritually broken by the dominant 1930s American culture that had such limited space for them. They had to make do with a few streets in Greenwich Village, with a few people not completely antagonistic and judgmental. If nothing else, this novel clarifies the nature of the victory gay people have enjoyed since the 1930s by showing the costs of being openly gay then.

The novel ends with Karel in a dangerous situation with the "beautifully sinister" Louis, a troublesome figure who has decided that he wants Karel's suit—the one Karel's wearing. Karel cries, and implores Louis to take mercy on him. Louis calls him a woman, and says he should save his tears, that he's not interested in them. When Gabriel, Louis's roommate, shows up, Karel is confused about what's going on. He "started to ask another question but looked pretty instead." Finally, after getting a bit of money from him, Louis again demands Karel's suit, Karel submits, and they fall into a kind of dark swoon, giving the story an obscure ending that must have seemed to its first readers to summarize the darkness and confusion of love and sex between men. "Louis leaned over and Karel saw him kissing him before he felt the bite. Then Karel screamed."

Ford was a gay original, bold and unashamed and productive from the beginning to the end, first as editor and publisher, later as novelist, poet, filmmaker, and visual artist. His influence on the gay culture that he lived in for most of his life will be made known gradually, as readers and scholars and historians uncover the full story of his life and the full importance of his work. For now, we have the fresh memory of a gay artist that was until recently still among us, quietly and steadily disseminating the complex, sometimes surreal, tender messages he seemed destined to pass down from some strange lofty place, out of the past and from the heart.

HART CRANE (1899–1932) was exactly the age I am now, almost to the day—thirty-two years and nine months, as I write this—when he jumped off a ship headed from Mexico to New York and drowned on April 27, 1932. I'd heard the well-known story of his suicide before I began reading Paul Mariani's 1999 biography, *The Broken Tower*, and as the weeks and then months passed and I still hadn't finished the medium-length book (though I carried it with me everywhere, including on a wintertime trip to southern Florida during which I unknowingly drove by the spot where, ten miles out to sea, the ship was sailing when Crane leaped overboard), I gradually came to realize that I was putting off reading about the end of his life. There is something about Hart Crane's suicide that troubles me. Not that I entertain thoughts of suicide myself (though I have had such thoughts), or feel that I am *like him* in any strangely significant way (although, like him, I am struggling to be a writer, I come from Ohio, I'm gay, usually strapped for money, and have been prone to addictions). But I have never been so bothered by knowing about anyone else's suicide—not Sylvia Plath's, or Hemingway's, or even that of a young gay man from my hometown who, when we were both teenagers, I intimately knew. I feel, about Crane, that he shouldn't have done it. I feel that he still had work to do, and should have found a way out of his depression (and the Depression) and a way back to his work. It's as if I want to find some strength in him that he simply didn't have.

Five days before he died, in the last letter he wrote—there was no suicide note—to his stepmother, Crane sounds annoyed with the Mexicans, among whom he'd been living and seeking inspiration for

nearly eight months, and generally distraught and stressed and lonely, but he gives no hint of suicide. He informs her that she should watch for a crate of books he sent ahead, and tells her that he will call from New York (at night, when the rates are lower), where he wants to stop briefly to see some friends, and that he'll see her soon, and hopes to be useful to her—his father had died, and Crane hoped to salvage some of the family business, of which she was temporarily in charge. He does not come across as cheerful, but neither does he strike a note of *despair*. In the last sentence of the letter, he assures her, before signing off "Lovingly," that he'll "rest up on the boat."

Four days later, on the eve of his death, he sent a postcard to a friend: "Very pleasant journey," he says. "Shall write when I get in the upper latitudes." Did he—the poet who'd written only one good poem in more than two years—mean something cryptic by that line? Did he plan his suicide? Was the journey "pleasant" because he knew it would be his last?

His last poem, "The Broken Tower," composed in the months just before his death, is by far Crane's most memorable lyric, filled as it is with images of irreparable damage and yet a craving for full-throated expression. It opens:

> The bell-rope that gathers God at dawn
> Dispatches me as though I dropped down the knell
> Of a spent day—to wander the cathedral lawn
> From pit to crucifix, feet chill on steps from hell.

The ending of the forty-line poem is far from hopeless—it still sings the old Whitmanesque song of American rapture, a song that is transcendent of every dogma and every class, sexuality, and prosaic emotion (yet is somehow still unmistakably American).

> . . . —visible wings of silence sown
> In azure circles, widening as they dip
> The matrix of the heart, lift down the eye
> That shrines the quiet lake and swells a tower . . .
> The commodious, tall decorum of that sky
> Unseals her earth, and lifts love in its shower.

The First Time I Met Frank O'Hara

Crane, like most reasonably healthy people who commit suicide, must have had several reasons for killing himself (including, perhaps, biochemical depression that is now—but was not then—treatable), if it makes any sense to speak of *reasons* for a suicide at all. If we'd been able to ask him why he was going to do it, I imagine he would have not said anything at all, but rather given an evasive, hopeless shrug. His father—ironically the inventor of Life Savers candies—died fairly poor less than a year before his son did. Crane had been estranged from his mother for at least four years before his father's death brought them briefly together again. The man he came closest to loving, Emil Opffer, had long disappeared from Crane's solitary life. (After meeting Opffer in 1924, Crane wrote ecstatically in a letter, "I have seen the Word made Flesh. I mean nothing less, and I know now that there is such a thing as indestructibility. In the deepest sense, where flesh became transformed through intensity of response to counter-response, where sex was beaten out, where a purity of joy was reached that included tears.") Crane's other lovers were mostly sailors and anonymous, working-class boys.

At Christmastime, 1931, Crane embarked upon an affair with Peggy Cowley, an old friend, recently divorced from the critic Malcolm Cowley, another friend. By all accounts, they did have a sex life together for a while in Mexico, though Crane never abandoned his nocturnal visits to the docks and alleys, and he was apparently beaten aboard the ship he jumped from for propositioning a cabin boy early on the morning he died. It would be crude and surely wrong to say that a woman drove him to suicide; but Peggy probably was the first woman he'd ever slept with. After he had given heterosexuality an honest try, with a woman he knew well and probably even loved, perhaps Crane's forced acceptance of his homosexuality—at a time when being gay was heavily loaded with seriously negative connotations—was an unbearable source of pain that, in combination with his belief that he was failing as a poet, was incapable of earning a living, was an uncontrollable alcoholic, and was in some profound sense permanently alone in the world, made jumping drunkenly off the side of a ship into the sea an attractively desperate measure. Someone on the ship said she saw him swimming "strongly" after he'd jumped, as if he still wasn't sure he wanted to die.

Crane had often invoked suicide in his letters as an option during bad times. In April 1926, he was living in the country with some friends, Allen Tate and his wife, Caroline Gordon. He'd been invited by them to stay there for a while when he was broke and needed a quiet, safe place to live. While there, in Patterson, New York, he came into some money via the largesse of a generous patron, the banker Otto H. Kahn—and that was the beginning of the end of his friendly relations with the Tates. Their accusations were vague: they seemed to resent his undisciplined, "romantic" way of life; he didn't keep regular hours; he was a bad influence on them. Crane admitted that he was a "barbarian in many ways," but he refused to defend himself against such absurd charges the Tates made as that he wanted "to exploit [his] friends as menial servants" for fear of "offering [them] a deeper insult" than they offered him. He opened a long letter to his mother just after receiving the offending notes from his housemates:

Dear Grace:
It would be a relief to be able to talk with you an hour or so today.
I'm in such an uncertain position in regard to a number of things

that I feel as though it would be a fitting end to settle it with
powder and bullet.

If Crane thought seriously of suicide at such times, he would probably have been contemplating what the French sociologist Emile
Durkheim would have labeled an "egoistic" suicide. Durkheim
sought in his 1897 study *Le Suicide* to understand the act as the
result of social—rather than psychological—dilemmas. Within
Durkheim's system of thought on the subject, Crane's early thoughts
of suicide might have been due to his alienation from his various
"groups"—poets, homosexuals, family, friends. When he felt
rejected by a group—when he felt unsupported, friendless, without
the possibility of finding a lover, or when he felt that his power as a
poet, or his credibility as a human being, was lost—he may have
thought about killing himself. But if he did think about it at such
times, he—like most of us—was able to reinsert himself into some
group or another by apologizing to his friends, or finding new ones,
or writing another poem, or finding a new lover, or reconnecting
with his parents.

Durkheim's other two types of suicide are the "altruistic," who
*over*identifies with a group and feels that he has failed them, as in
Japanese hara-kiri and wartime heroism; and the "anomic," a person
whose social position changes drastically and who is suddenly, permanently (or so it would seem) without *any* social class after having
been accustomed to living comfortably within at least one.

When Crane committed suicide in 1932, he had, in some sense,
been removed from *all* of the groups that meant anything to him. By
making public his affair with Peggy Cowley, he was renouncing his
homosexuality (or trying to); and he felt that his ability to write

poetry had abandoned him. He was close to no one in his family and most of his friendships had been broken apart. As a raging alcoholic, perhaps he also felt that he was barely a legitimate member of the large class of "civilized" people. He must have felt profoundly alone, and he must have felt that there was no group to which he wished to belong that would accept him in his ruined, stricken state. The word *anomie* derives from the Greek word for *lawlessness*; it came to have its modern meaning from Durkheim's use of it to refer to behavior ungoverned by norms. *Webster's* defines the word as "social instability resulting from a breakdown of standards and values; also: personal unrest, alienation, and uncertainty that comes from a lack of purpose or ideals."

Crane's only purpose was to be a great poet, and his only ideals were those of poetic beauty and originality. In a 1924 letter to his mother and grandmother in which the poet attempts to persuade them of both his love for them and the necessity of pursuing his work, even if it should take him away from them, he writes: "... the freedom of my imagination is the most precious thing that life holds for me,—and the only reason I can see for living." Earlier that year, in another letter to his mother, Crane had written from New York (which he called "this bronco-busting city") some lines that give us a clue to just how entirely he identified himself as a poet. "How strange it seems to me sometimes to be gradually meeting and talking with all the names [that is, the poets living in New York] that I used to wonder over years ago,—and to find how, in most cases, I am valued as an individual—for the attributes most natural to myself. It does give me more confidence than I ever thought I should have." That he should be accepted into the rarefied circle of New York poets—that, and nothing else, gave Crane confidence in himself.

The First Time I Met Frank O'Hara

When Crane's long poem *The Bridge* was published in 1930, most of the reviews were devastating, including several by poets he had considered close friends. This wholesale, ruthless criticism must have made him feel completely rejected by that circle of poets he had once so eagerly solicited. Additionally, he had become known to many as a sorry, violent alcoholic who lost control of himself more often than not and was seldom good company or a good friend after about 1929. Crane went to jail more than once, and he never went there for a glamorous or political crime; he went because he was drunk and a noisy nuisance. Lincoln Kirstein, in a 1982 essay, remembered having met Crane a few times: "He never failed to frighten me. His reputation, of course, preceded him, a negative fame of lurid pyrotechnics, at once alluring and repulsive."

It seems Hart Crane was never happy for long. He grew up in Cleveland, the only child of a bitterly unhappy couple who finally divorced when their only child was seventeen. In a letter to Grace, his mother, dated December 21, 1923, the young poet wrote from Woodstock, New York:

> ... One can live happily on very little, I have found, if the mind and spirit have some definite objective in view. I expect I'll always have to drudge for my living, and I'm quite willing to always do it, but I am no more fooling myself that the mental bondage and spiritual bondage of the more remunerative sorts of work is worth the sacrifices inevitably involved. If I can't continue to create the sort of poetry that is my intensest and deepest component in life—then it all means very little to me, and then I might as well tie myself up to some snug ambition and "success" (the common idol that every Tom Dick and Harry is bowing to everywhere).

Then, in the same letter, he goes deeper, and approaches the painful subject of his *other* big difference from his mother and most other people. For Crane, it seems, "certain ardours" he felt within himself were simultaneously poetic and homoerotic; the "fight" to be himself and to know himself was both artistic and psychosexual in nature.

> ... I don't know whether it is possible for all people to understand certain ardours that I have, and perhaps there is no special reason why you, as my mother, should understand that side of me any better than most people. As I have said, I am perfectly willing to be misunderstood, but I don't want to put up any subterfuges before your understanding of me if I can help it. You didn't follow certain convictions that you had when you were my age because it wasn't easy enough; and I know what strong obstacles were put in your way. I, too, have had to fight a great deal just to be myself and know myself at all, and I think I have been doing and am doing a great deal in following out certain natural and innate directions in myself. By Jove—I don't know of much else that is worth the having in our lives.

New York City was for Crane a relief and a revelation—he discovered that he wasn't so queer after all, or at least that he wasn't the only one. He was, rather, part of an appealing, interesting group. New York approved as no one in Cleveland had of his ambition to be an artist rather than the scion of a (then) successful businessman. Crane succeeded in having his poems published in New York journals; he met writers and painters, and had long conversations about things he cared about; he saw the Brooklyn Bridge, which became a permanent symbol for him of miraculous, man-made connection; and he found lovers and friends, and, for a while at least, accepted his homosexuality as a part of his personality. It's hard to say unequivocally of Crane that anything he experienced was *good* for him, since so much of his life was filled with a tragic suffering and sadness, and it ended so badly—but he would never have become the poet he was had he not come to New York. "The Tunnel," from the long poem named after the bridge that went from Manhattan to where he often lived, Brooklyn Heights, is a tribute to the New York City subway and the lively characters he encountered underground.

> Performances, assortments, résumés—
> Up Times Square to Columbus Circle lights
> Channel the congresses, nightly sessions,
> Refractions of the thousand theatres, faces—
> Mysterious kitchens. . . . You shall search them all.
> Someday by heart you'll learn each famous sight
> And watch the curtain lift in hell's despite;
> You'll find the garden in the third act dead,
> Finger your knees—and wish yourself in bed
> With tabloid crime-sheets perched in easy sight.

But even in New York, where Crane probably lived his happiest—or his least miserable—days, his mental state was never secure and he almost never gives an indication in letters (and certainly not in his poetry) of feeling comfortable or serene for long, though he did have moments of blissful good feeling. His letters show us a young man (who often doesn't seem so young) filled with contradictory thoughts, both high and low at the same time, hopeful and pessimistic, lost and found. In his first letter to his father, when Crane was seventeen and living alone in New York for the first time, he writes: "It is a great shock, but a good tonic, to come down here as I have and view the countless multitudes. It seems sometimes almost as though you had lost yourself, and were trying vainly to find somewhere in this sea of humanity, your lost identity."

In his next letter, again to his father, six days later, his search for himself has taken off, and he uses a word to describe his ambition that he will use again fifteen years later, in his last written document, the postcard quoted above: "I realize more entirely every day, that I am preparing for a fine life: that I have powers, which, if correctly balanced, will enable me to mount to extraordinary latitudes." For now, he suggests, he will focus on climbing up within himself in order to do his work. "There is constantly an inward struggle, but the time to worry is only when there is no inward debate, and consequently there is smooth sliding to the devil." In 1932, the "inward debate" would cease. But in 1917, it was raging inside of him full force. "There is only one harmony, that is the equilibrium maintained by two opposite forces, equally strong." Among the forces working against each other inside the young Hart Crane was that of his body versus his mind; his homosexuality against the knowledge that being gay would bring him endless grief. "We all get to thinking that our heads are really our bodies, and most of the time go floating around with only our brain conscious, forgetting that our bodies have requirements also." Crane in New York was finding that he wasn't able to live a purely intellectual or artistic life if that had to mean a life disconnected from his sexuality—the two, for him, were not just equally important, but identical. "Sterility," he wrote in a letter to the editors of the *Little Review*, "is the only 'decadence' I recognize."

Crane was also tortured by other opposed forces: the crass capitalism of his father versus his own artistic ambitions, somewhat paralleled in the sight of his father forever battling Grace, who at least for a while supported Crane's literary longings; the city (and its sexy distractions) versus the country (where he could focus on working); the poetic vision of grim apocalypse in the influential T. S. Eliot's "The Wasteland" (published in 1922) versus Crane's own wishful vision of achieved optimism ("I am interested in possibilities," he wrote); and the endless quandary of being alone versus being among people or with a lover. At nineteen, back in Cleveland, he writes to a friend, "Of course I am utterly alone,—want to be,—and am beginning to rather enjoy the slippery scales-of-the-fish, continual escape, attitude." Just a few lines later, in the same letter: "My Akron friend [a young male lover] has not been able to see me for some five weeks, and I am in need of a balm, spiritual and fleshly." Crane was a nervous, anxious person, and his comforts were drinking, literature, music, friendship, and men. Reading and writing, after drinking, were Crane's most reliable balms, and he took them both seriously. "I need time (a natural requirement with me for all writing or thought) to sit Buddha-like for a couple of hours every day and let things sift themselves into some semblance of order in my brain." There were within Crane the opposing feelings of a great, sublime literary power and its imminent demise, a fatal draining-away of all that was good within him. "At times," he writes in June 1922, "I feel an enormous power in me—that seems almost supernatural.... I have known moments in eternity." By December of that same year, perhaps with Eliot's new poem in mind, he confessed, "Life is meagre with me. I am unsatisfied and left always begging for beauty. I am tied to the stake—a little more wastefully burnt every day of my life...."

‹◊›

In an essay by Crane's friend Allen Tate (himself a poet and critic) that was written shortly after Crane's death and revised in 1937, we find the first attempt to place Crane in the context of literary history—as the last romantic, questing poet at the end of a line that goes back through Whitman, Shelley, and Keats, to Dante. "Crane not only ends the romantic era in his own person; he ends it logically and morally. Beyond Crane no future poet can go. . . . Beyond the quest of pure sensation and its ordering symbolism lies the total destruction of art. By attempting an extreme solution of the romantic problem Crane proved that it cannot be solved." Tate was one of many critics who judged the bulk of Hart Crane's poetry a failure. He thought "The Bridge" a poem with "no inherent content," and that the poet had plunged into "sentimentality and chaos." For me, Crane's poetry, while difficult and sometimes obscure, is at least an expression of poetic aspiration *ad astra*—and it is certainly unique linguistic music. His "project," according to Harold Bloom's introduction to a new edition of Crane's *Complete Poems*, was "in renewal of Whitman's: to fuse the myth of America with a realized homoeroticism." Crane was among the gay American writers for whom sexuality was a deep force that acted strictly and powerfully under the surface of his work, exerting a steady and irresistible influence upon both the writer's choice of subject matter and his style. There is a turbulence to Crane's work—a strong current of disorder and opacity— that is the direct result of his sexuality. He was thrown into disorder because being gay was, on some level, unacceptable to him due partly to the fact that it was unacceptable to others, including his parents. His sexuality was clouded because it never quite realized itself in love—he never got a full view of his sexuality, even during his best moments with Emil Opffer, because he never enjoyed a long-term, mutually loving, open and honest relationship with a man, a situation he seems always to have longed for. That he *was* able to achieve a fusion of the myth of America that Bloom mentions with a "realized homoeroticism" is a measure of his power as an *artist*, not as a human being with a particularly strong libido to which he was often painfully powerless. As a man, he took some pleasure from being gay, but he mostly suffered from it; as a poet, he was able to thrive on the tension his sexuality built up within him—for a while.

If Crane had been born fifty years later, and had been comfortable with living openly, evenly proudly, as a gay man, he probably would not have died at thirty-two. But his poetry, too, would have been very different. So much of his sensibility as a poet seems to derive from the partial, refracted, condensed disclosure of what is hidden, even impacted, within him, some of which, at least, is profoundly relevant to his homosexuality, that it is hard to imagine him writing without that sense of struggle that characterizes his best work. Crane was among the least prolific of great poets. For him, writing a poem took enormous mental and emotional effort and was of great consequence: he knew, when he was working well, that he was making an important work of art *and* that he was handling and witnessing pieces of himself that had never come out before.

Hart Crane's poems are like strange, aloof, ghostly visitors who have sublimely eloquent, sinister phrases that they utter whenever approached, a spooky answer to every kind of question. "It is the unbetrayable reply," Crane wrote at the end of "Voyages," his only love poem, "Whose accent no farewell can know."

GLENWAY WESCOTT (1901-1987) was blessed at an early age: beautiful, intelligent, successful, and the author in 1940 of a one hundred-page novel, *The Pilgrim Hawk*, that is nothing short of a masterpiece ("this great American novel" belongs, according to Susan Sontag, "among the treasures of twentieth-century American literature"). Wescott knew many of the most interesting people of his day, lived in Paris when that was the place to be, had plenty of both sex and love, and lived a long, healthy, reasonably happy life.

When he was only nineteen, Glenway met and fell in love with the man he would live with until the end of his life, Monroe Wheeler, who became an important figure at the Museum of Modern Art in New York. In 1929, Wheeler formed a business partnership with Barbara Harrison, a wealthy heiress from California; they called their enterprise Harrison of Paris and produced deluxe editions of works by Shakespeare, Byron, and Wescott, among others. The unprofitable company did not last for long, but Harrison married Wescott's brother, Lloyd, and she made it easy for the entire Wescott family to never have any serious worries about money. She was also the model for Wescott's fictional Alexandra Henry, at whose home the action turns in *The Pilgrim Hawk*. Between Harrison and Wheeler, Glenway was able to live in high style both in New York, where Wheeler always had an elegant apartment, and in the New Jersey countryside, where Harrison financed a large farm. Wescott was for several years president of the American Academy-Institute of Arts and Letters; among his close friends were Somerset Maugham, Marianne Moore,

The First Time I Met Frank O'Hara

Katherine Anne Porter, Paul Cadmus, the Sitwells, Philippe and Pauline de Rothschild, Thornton Wilder, George Platt Lynes, Alfred Kinsey, and Colette. Though Wescott was troubled by his inability to finish another novel after *The Apartment in Athens* (which was a bestseller) in 1945, a selection from his journals was published posthumously as *Continual Lessons*, and it too (like *The Pilgrim Hawk*) is miraculously good, as if the gods were determined to give their favored boy one last benediction. Now a new biography (Jerry Rosco's 2002 *Glenway Wescott Personally*) sets all these happy facts down for the record, and complicates them.

Most writers work for years to achieve a modicum of success. Wescott didn't have to struggle much at all in the beginning; his struggles came later. Though his first novel, *The Apple of the Eye*, was not an enormous hit when it was published in 1924, there was a blurb by Sinclair Lewis on the jacket announcing that the book had about it "something curiously like genius." Three years later, Wescott's second novel, *The Grandmothers*, was a bestseller about the Midwest that Louis Bromfield called "one of the most beautiful books I have ever read." A collection of stories and an essay, published together as *Goodbye, Wisconsin* the next year, kept Wescott's name, for a few years, among the best known in American letters. In 1930, Harrison of Paris published Wescott's final work set in the Midwest, and in 1932 he published a book of essays; in the same year he produced a light, illustrated work about failed saints. Then he dried up for several years. Gertrude Stein wrote of him in her *Autobiography of Alice B. Toklas*: "He has a certain syrup but it does not pour." It poured occasionally, when the weather was right, but not very often.

⟨◊⟩

Wescott and Wheeler sometimes shared boyfriends, beginning with the most important of them all, George Platt Lynes. The sharing was never equal or easy. Rosco tells the story of Lynes's first appearance on the scene. When he arrived at the hotel where Wescott and Wheeler were sharing a room, Wheeler was out, and Wescott was alone. "The first time we met," Wescott is quoted to have said, "he picked up a photo of Monroe [Wheeler] that was in our room and gave a whistle. And I thought, 'Uh, oh.'" What is remarkable is that this ménage, and others involving younger men later on, worked so well for all involved. There was far less jealousy and resentment than there might have been, and more honesty and mutual care and thoughtfulness than is common. The story of Wheeler and Wescott together is never simple, and never dull, and there are hints in the biography of some real unhappiness between them at times, but the couple stands out, in the end, as one of the great gay unions of the twentieth century. They were still together, after all, when Wescott died.

After 1945, Wescott's productivity and success as a writer came more or less permanently to an end. He had two bestsellers and a literary classic under his belt, and he sometimes worked at producing another novel, but apart from a collection of essays published in 1962 as *Images of Truth*, he turned out very little new material, much to his and Wheeler's chagrin. It's disturbing to know that by the 1970s Wescott was reduced to writing an essay for a literary anthology about the breath of bulls, a worn-out bathrobe, and the loss of his favorite fountain pen. Rosco does his best to put a smiling face on Wescott's old age, but the final chapters of the biography are a little disheartening. That said, however, Rosco reports that Wescott did note in a datebook late in his life, "I have learned more from being happy than from any of my misfortunes or sorrows."

The First Time I Met Frank O'Hara

Wescott considered himself something of a literary failure, despite the commercial success of *The Grandmothers* in 1927 and *Apartment in Athens* in 1945 and the lasting literary acclaim of *The Pilgrim Hawk*, which has never been out of print for long. "All my life," he wrote in a letter to his brother in 1949, "I have had to force myself to write; sitting at my desk somewhat longer than anyone else has to, in grim determination and concentration, waiting and waiting to feel my talent...."

<>

The Pilgrim Hawk: A Love Story is the story of an afternoon visit by a wealthy Irish married couple, the Cullens—and Mrs. Cullen's full-grown falcon, which perches hooded on her wrist when they arrive and throughout much of the novel—to the home of the narrator's close friend and future sister-in-law in France. Mr. Cullen's complex feelings of hatred, jealousy, and fear of his wife's beloved bird—she is obsessively (and literally) attached to it—form the emotional core of the novel. Upon their arrival at the house, Cullen explains to Alwyn Tower, the narrator, that they could scarcely have left the bird behind: "The most awful things happen if we leave her in the hotel. She frightens the chambermaids, and they scream and weep." And besides, Mrs. Cullen thought that Alexandra Henry, the young heiress in and around whose country house the story is set, would like to see the bird. Mrs. Cullen, we learn later in the novel, is not actually Irish like her husband; she's English. "Britannia rules the waves and so on," her husband says.

They are, strangely enough, in love with each other, this unhappy and restless couple. Though he is richer than she is, she "had money of her own," and it is never suggested that her devotion to him is mercenary or corrupt. Their life together as a married couple, however, is depicted by Wescott as very strange and very dark—the novel is among other things the devastating picture of a type of heterosexual unhappiness. It's also a meditation on drinking, loneliness, sexual appetite, and the difficulty of knowing for sure what one wants from other people. But as Wescott once wrote, ascribing his idea to Balzac, "what interests one in a novel, in the last analysis, is the quantity of glimpsed detail, the asides and the incidents along the way; not the over-all turn of events or the holocaust at the close or the happy ending." Though the holocaust or happy ending—it's hard to say which it is—at the close of *The Pilgrim Hawk* is riveting and memorable, it is in fact the glimpsed detail spread evenly through the writing, from beginning to end, that makes this novel so powerful and important.

There may be no truer portrayal in fiction of a besotted, jealous husband than that of Larry Cullen. There is nothing simple about Wescott's description of him, which begins upon the Cullens' arrival. "He was a large man, not really fat but with bulk and softness irregularly here and there, not so much in the middle as up and down his back, all around his head, in his hands. His British complexion suggested eating and drinking rather than hunting and shooting; certainly nothing about him suggested hawking. His hazel eyes were a little bloodshot, wavering golden now and then; and he had a way of opening and shutting his lips, like an unsympathetic pout, or a dispirited kiss, under the tufts of his mustache." Tower spends a great deal of time with Cullen as the action moves forward, and he gets an intimate look at the man, who proves tragically weak and flawed, though not at all a passive victim or total dupe or cuckold. He loves his wife, and she loves him. That is the central mystery of the story—why do they love each other? He is unattractive in so many ways, physically and otherwise; he's cowardly at times, drinks and eats far too much, is not clever or amusing, and hates his wife's favorite things, from her political affiliations to the ubiquitous bird that messily eats raw, bloody pigeon and shits on the finest floors in Europe with impunity. The narrator is particularly fascinated by Cullen's alcoholic voracity; the Irishman seems eager to drink himself into a totally different kind of existence, in which wildness and chaos would seem to take over in place of anything resembling responsibility and compliance to his wife's wishes. The narrator's— or Wescott's—reflections on this lumbering, foolish man getting very drunk before dinner lead him to some reckless speculation of his own and some of the finest writing by any gay American novelist.

Perhaps at other times, I reminded myself, his character was ideal; his mind vigorous; his great physique fresh and energetic. That would explain the love his wife bore him. Suppose you have learned to like or to love such a man when he was sober; and you happen to dislike him when he is not; and he doesn't know the difference or can't help it. The temptation to interfere, the fond hope of reformation, must be very great. Thus I began to think indulgently of Mrs. Cullen's selfish nervousness and sharp tongue. Although, if what I had seen that afternoon was the worst of it, certainly she exaggerated and overemphasized the plight she was in with him. An ordinary boring conceited uneasy childish man! Yet out of his petty instability she seemed to expect something odious or dangerous to develop any minute—as if she felt the ground underfoot move a bit, like a landslide starting, and caught glimpses of little creeping sickening things close to the surface, coming up! Love itself is an exaggeration, and very likely to lead to others.

Cullen's wife proves at least equally complex. Her appearance changes with each episode of the novel—in the end, she is nearly hysterical and wild, like her hawk. But at the start she is a stylish, rich woman who is nothing if not civilized. When she arrives at the house in a large chauffeured car, her husband and the driver attend her. "She was dressed with extreme elegance and she wore the highest heels I ever saw, on which, with one solicitous male at each elbow, she stumbled across the ancient cobblestones, the bird swaying a little and hunching its wings to steady itself." After the climax of the novel (in which a gun is brandished but never used), when her love for Cullen has been tested and she has proven her capacity for tolerating his most extreme symptoms of jealousy without loss of love—and without forcing a change in their lives—Madeleine Cullen emerges as a rugged heroine, a lone soldier who is forever fighting on behalf of a form of love that she seems to accept as her cause by default.

From our viewpoint, behind her, seeing her through the sunset-streaked window, against the background of the old park and the shrubs and the gray pond with ripples unclosing away from the place where the gun had gone down, Mrs. Cullen was beautiful. Throughout her somewhat bulky body—motherly torso and panting breast and round neck—there was wonderful strength; and between her absurd high heels and her fist in the rough glove, there was exact perpendicularity: the yard-wind wings now settling back on top. And the fact that she looked a bit ridiculous,

disheveled and second-rate and past her prime, made it all the finer, I thought, as she turned and came slowly back indoors.

The "glimpsed detail" in these passages is remarkable, from the bloodshot, hazel eyes of Mr. Cullen, to the high heels stumbling on ancient cobblestones, to the mysterious bird hunching its wings and the gun thrown in the pond sending ripples "unclosing away." This level of significant observation is maintained in nearly every sentence of the book. Some of it is comical, such as after Alex recalls a feast in Tangier and then mentions, for the first time, dinner, which as it happens is to be the same food as the bird will get: "The reminiscence of the brandied wild pig, the prospect of *pigeons aux groseilles,* charmed Cullen; you could see the gourmandise shining on his rosy lips." Alex suggests a walk outdoors, and Cullen agrees to go, "though his appetite did not need whetting. 'By Jove,' he said, 'I do look forward to those squabs.'"

All of Wescott's wry observations in this novel are tinged with a shade of melancholic, riding-into-the-darkness fear. There's always the feeling that, for the people in this love story, nothing is ever predictable, or even stable or reliable. When the foursome go out for their walk in the park adjacent to Alexandra's property, the narrator sees something in the arrangement of the trees that's reminiscent of human relations, but safer. "The way they stood in informal groups, or in line, or alone at a little distance, seemed not only to conform to the art of parks but to express their feelings about each other: idiosyncrasies of affection or obedience, pride or pain. And unlike human characters in such an assembly, they promised or threatened nothing more; no episodes or developments."

Threatened episodes and developments—the prospect of things undergoing a radical reversal or change—are what the two real main characters of the book, Alexandra and Alwyn, argue over in their subtle and intricate communication with each other. For her, the high drama that appears to be the natural result of love between a man and woman, is acceptable, even desirable—perhaps. In a line that summons decades of interest in psychoanalytic theory when it was still relatively new and promising as a means of escaping rotten routines and mindless repeated mistakes, Alwyn points out what should be, he thinks, for Alexandra, the afternoon's meaning: "Fantastic bad object lessons." But she'll have none of his moralizing precaution. Her betrayal of some shade of ambivalence about her heedlessness, though, is the final image of this dazzling novel, and, historically, among the most memorable moments in a tradition of gay literature that thrived on not stating its intentions explicitly.

‹◊›

The Pilgrim Hawk gives a complex view of one man with an uneasy but viable alternative to conventional, heterosexual love. "His," to quote Sontag again, "is the arid wisdom of a profoundly unmarried consciousness." The perspective he has devised seems both necessary and surprisingly suitable for him, especially when his way is contrasted with that of the Cullens. The narrator never quite says what his way of being consists of; he does say that he has been "lucky in love," but there are also signs that he suffers from sexual hunger. "Youthfulness persists, alas," he says, "long after one has ceased to be young. Love-life goes on indefinitely, with less and less likelihood of being loved, less and less ability to love, and the stomach-ache of love still as sharp as ever. The old bachelor is like an old hawk." Whatever it is—and since we know that Wescott was gay, I infer that the Wescott-like narrator is, too—Alwyn Tower's *aim* is to have a simpler, more mutually loving love life, or to put it another way, to find better object lessons than the usual ones offered by fucked-up straight people—or anyone else—circa 1939.

There must be, Tower seems to be thinking but is too polite to say aloud, some method by which a person can circumvent the madness of jealousy. "Morally speaking," Tower says near the end of his observations, "those Cullens had crowded me out of myself." Which, I suppose, is what the Cullens of the world (both gay and straight) will always do, given the chance to impose themselves on a person who lives in such a way that he or she is looking for the right way to live. The thrill of *The Pilgrim Hawk* is the knowledge, slowly and skeptically gained, that there is always a *completely different* way of living from that of the struggling and occasionally beautiful but foolish people that underestimate the value of the straightforward expression, the self-exposing gesture, and the humbling aspects of being in love and, especially, of being loved.

The Pilgrim Hawk is the kind of novel that leads any reader to wonder about his or her own feelings, beliefs, and aspirations in the realm of love between two people. When Alexandra tells Alwyn on the very last page of the novel that she envies the Cullens, and he concludes "from the look on her face that she herself did not quite know whether she meant it," the meaning of the novel is set as a kind of spiraling question about how much it's worth to be in love with and loved by the same person. The Cullens are, in so many ways, far from enviable; they are violently unstable, and their love for each other seems to persist almost despite the way they behave with each other. They are an example of the kind of couple one hopes not to become; but they *are* a couple.

I have lately found myself to be seriously coupled for the first time in many years, after a long stretch of detachment and promiscuous wandering. Just as I've been told by friends and warned by books like *The Pilgrim Hawk*, there are challenges to intimacy for which I could not have been prepared. The resistance I put up to my lover takes many forms: it is physical, emotional, sexual, psychological, even philosophical. There have been times when I would have considered us to be about as enviable as the Cullens, with their big symbolical bird between them and their sorry stories of scouring the world for something to do that would hold their interest for a long weekend. But I know that that hawk—that fantastic bad object lesson—is the representation of a point on an abstract continuum that exists, in its way, for every couple. Everyone's lover has a pilgrim hawk that gets more attention than it deserves or requires.

But the unspoken wish that Wescott's writing whispers to us throughout his middle-aged novel is, perhaps, that two lovers might agree, in time, upon the importance and the meaning of what is between them, contriving thereby to transform the object into a symbol not of captivity or usurpation but of shared feeling and mutual love. Not every pilgrim hawk is tethered to one wrist; some symbols are shared; and some pilgrim hawks, if encouraged, will eventually just fly away.

ON THE DAY OF HER WEDDING, February 21, 1938, the fabulous and troubled Jane Auer became the legendary Jane Bowles (1917-1973). She would turn twenty-one the next day. An indisputably great and understated wit, known among her friends as a lively, liberated, sophisticated young woman, she had already endured years of pain and discomfort due to "tuberculosis of the knee," the result of an accident in which she fell from a horse and broke her leg. She spent two years as a teenager in a Swiss sanatorium and had an operation on the knee that left her with a permanent limp and chronic pain. Her father had died when she was just thirteen, and she lived mostly with her high-strung, neurotic mother. The two of them moved back to New York City (where Jane had been born) from Long Island shortly after the death of Jane's father.

Their first new address in the city was the Croydon Hotel on East Eighty-sixth Street, where young Jane had her first "crushes" on women, particularly female singers, one of whom, Frances Williams, lived in the hotel. Another, Frances Faye, was the most inspired lesbian cabaret performer of all time. Her only live recording, "Caught in the Act," has her, well into middle age, introducing her next song with a dry joke: "When I first heard this song I was having a malted at the Croydon bar. . . ." The Croydon bar was not, Faye implied, the kind of place where a person would have a malted; quite the contrary. Her joke suggests that the Croydon bar in the 1930s was a smoky, sexy, adult environment, and it seems appropriate that Jane Bowles, who must have been a strangely grown-up sixteen-year-old, lived upstairs.

It was in Manhattan, a few years later, that Jane met and married Paul Bowles. Paul, who was bisexual, was perplexed by Jane's refusal to sleep with him, but they liked each other, and she was conveniently to come into some money when she married. They agreed to think of marriage as little more than an "amusing" romp anyway, a romp that turned out, however, to last until the end of Jane's life thirty-five years later. The composer David Diamond, a close friend of Jane's at the time, remembers having a long talk with her before the wedding. He was trying to find out why she wanted to marry at all, since it seemed to him such a ludicrous decision. "I can still hear that soft purr of a voice saying, 'But honey, I'm so lonely.' And she limped off to get a cigarette."

For their honeymoon, the couple first went to Panama on a freighter, traveling with two wardrobe trunks, twenty-seven suitcases, a typewriter, and a record player. In a Panama City bookshop, Jane stole a copy of *The Young and Evil*, the then infamous novel by her friends Ford and Tyler. According to Paul, he and Jane got along well in Central America, though their sex life together failed to blossom. One night in Guatemala City, Jane went with some new friends to see her first brothel and was mistaken by the chief bodyguard of a major politician for a working girl. He tried to force his way with her, and she only narrowly escaped his passionate embrace. Typically, Paul had already gone back to the hotel to sleep alone.

The newlyweds went from Central America to Paris, where the real trouble between them began to brew. Jane quickly found a society of lesbians in Paris, and she preferred their company, particularly late at night, even to that of the most famous stars of the art world and Paul, who at the time was at the beginning of his first career, that of a successful composer (his second career, as a writer, later eclipsed hers). But she and Paul kept traveling together as they would do for much of their lives, first with the money she inherited, later with money earned from books and articles by both of them, and commission fees for Paul's music. They went on during this first long trip to Cannes and to Eze-Village, where they rented a house on the Mediterranean. It was there that Jane began to speak to Paul of her mystical ideas about women and men. Men, she told him, "are all on the outside, not interesting. They have no mystery. Women are profound and mysterious—and obscene." She told Paul of an encounter she had just had in which she performed oral sex on a man to earn money to buy clothes for a woman she'd met. "It didn't mean a thing," she said. "There's nothing disgusting about men," Paul remembered her saying. Then, he told Jane's biographer, she added, "in an almost religious way, 'There *is* something disgusting about women.'" And, he must have understood her to imply, there was for her something profoundly attractive, even irresistible, about women, too.

It was around this time that Jane was writing her only novel and her masterpiece, *Two Serious Ladies*, which Knopf published successfully in the United States in 1943. There is something oddly apt, as with so many of the circumstances of Jane's life, about the fact that the roiling years of the Second World War were Jane's happiest by far. Yet even these years were deeply ambivalent times for her, and she was already showing signs of the mental distress that she was the first to make light of. She was obsessed with writing but considered herself a failure; she was notoriously indecisive about everything from settling on a literary project to the evening's dinner plans; and she found more agony and discomfort than pleasure from her affairs with women. Much of her work, especially the novel, consists of fantastic, desperate-seeming attempts to both express and mock her conflicted, anguished, often paralyzing mental states. Like many other artists working around the time of the war, and like many homosexual writers past and present, Jane Bowles found an ironic stance toward her material to be the only one she could sustain with any power of persuasion or effect of authority.

At the beginning of *Two Serious Ladies*, she comes right to the point, writing about the childhood of a character, Christina Goering, based, like the other serious lady of the novel, Frieda Copperfield, very clearly upon the author herself. "She was in the habit of going through many mental struggles—generally of a religious nature—and she preferred to be with other people and organize games. These games, as a rule, were very moral, and often involved God. However, no one else enjoyed them and she was obliged to spend a great part of the day alone." In this opening passage, many of the novel's cards are laid on the table and they will become major themes: habitual mental struggle, eccentric ideas about morality and religion, company versus solitude, and, above all, elements of jolting surprise and unpredictability. *Two Serious Ladies* is the flamboyant, bemusing story of two women struggling to "redeem" themselves by boldly facing their worst fears, which are of boredom, depression, and the idea that the world, though often terribly ordinary on the surface, is essentially alienating and hostile rather than settled and safe.

Christina Goering grows up to be a most unusual woman. On page eight of the novel, Bowles writes, "As a grown woman Miss Goering was no better liked than she had been as a child." She has few friends aside from Miss Gamelon, her "companion," who arrives unexpectedly one day on the suggestion of her cousin, who'd spoken of

Christina years before. Lucy Gamelon has nothing to do, so she stays with Christina, and they do nothing much together, since Christina has the luxury of a secure income, being the daughter of "an American industrialist of German parentage" and "a New York lady of a very distinguished family," somewhat, though not exactly, like Jane Bowles herself. (Her father was a successful insurance salesman whose parents were German and Austrian Jews; her mother was from a middle-class Jewish family that hailed from Long Island.)

Lucy Gamelon, the companion, says many things that could just as well have been said by her benefactress Christina Goering, except that Christina would probably say the opposite. For example, Lucy says, "I always believe . . . that you get your warning. Some people don't heed their warnings. That's when they come into conflict. I think that anything you feel strange or nervous about, you weren't cut out to do." Had Christina given her view of the same subject, she probably would have argued that one *must* do precisely what one feels strange or nervous about in order to prove its harmlessness. If a situation or a person is menacing, Christina might say, one must walk up to it, look it in the eyes and ask, in effect, Are you *really* so dangerous? If you don't confront it, you'll never know, and you'll live in endless fear and anxiety; you'll draw a dire conclusion that will render you depressed about the condition of the world and the intentions of people. Paul Valéry once turned a famous line by Pascal into another, related, idea by negating all the elements of the sentence. Pascal's confession that the eternal silence of infinite space filled him with dread became, instead, Valéry's observation that the intermittent racket of our little neighborhood reassures us. Jane Bowles and her characters busy themselves with making a reassuring, intermittent racket in order to avoid altogether the dreadful silence of infinite space.

The First Time I Met Frank O'Hara

Sometimes, of course, the scary object, or the infinite space, is not out in the world, but within oneself—as with feeling lonely or vaguely miserable. Christina Goering decides early in the novel to leave her large, comfortable home where she lives uneventfully along with Lucy and Arnold, an unhappy, overweight, charmless man who moves in shortly after Christina happens to meet him at a party. He invited her home with him that night and was surprised (along with the reader) when she accepted—and horrified when she was susceptible to his *father's* charms. Arnold falls awkwardly in love with Christina, and insinuates himself (easily enough) into the household. The threesome moves, after Christina's instigation, to a small, decrepit cottage on a dreary deserted island. Christina tries to explain her decision thus to exile the household to the appalled Lucy by referring to her "own little idea of salvation." "In my opinion," Miss Gamelon replies, "you could perfectly well work out your salvation during certain hours of the day without having to move everything." But Christina's mind is made up. "The idea," she says, "is to change first of our own volition and according to our own inner promptings before they impose completely arbitrary changes on us." Miss Gamelon has no such inner promptings, she says, "and I think you have a colossal nerve to identify yourself with anybody else at all. As a matter of fact, I think that if you leave this house, I shall give you up as a hopeless lunatic." But when Christina packs up and heads for the "tawdry" island shack, both Lucy and Arnold follow her like smitten disciples.

The story of Christina Goering and Lucy and Arnold and Arnold's father and various minor characters is interrupted by a long middle chapter about Christina's friend Frieda Copperfield, the other "serious lady" of the novel. Mrs. Copperfield is traveling with her husband in Central America, just as Jane and Paul Bowles did. She has a sultry affair with a young prostitute, Pacifica. She brings the girl home with her, and in the final scene of the novel she introduces Pacifica to Christina Goering, who is about to be abandoned by another worthless man who managed to pick her up due to her complete indifference to men in general and her obscure vision of redemption by confrontation.

The two women, in the final scene, make for a very odd couple, not at all like two serious ladies according to the usual meanings of those words. They're both struggling hard to be amusing and amused with each other, they're both pathetic, unwanted, undesirable, and drunk. As Mrs. Copperfield says, "I *have* gone to pieces, which is a thing I've wanted to do for years." In the end, Christina is alone, hope, she feels, having "discarded a childish form forever." She has made some spiritual progress, she seems to be thinking, and is "nearer to becoming a saint" than she was before because she has gone to the effort of examining herself in strange contexts and situations, faced fears and anxieties, and survived. It is possible, she admits, that a part of her that is hidden from her own view is "piling sin upon sin as fast as Mrs. Copperfield" is. "This latter possibility Miss Goering thought to be of considerable interest," in the last line of the novel, "but of no great importance."

‹◊›

Two Serious Ladies is, for me, among the central queer works of literary art. It expresses more perfectly than any other novel I can think of what it's like to be a sexual outsider with the belief, "of a religious nature," that there is significance—and a state of grace, so to speak—to be gleaned from the experience of being gay. We don't depend on this belief for our survival—we all depend on more basic instincts for that—but it can become the predominant quest in a life devoted to self-knowledge and self-perfection, in the Wildean sense of making one's life a work of art. The beauty of it, in a way, is the fact that though it may be "of considerable interest," it is nonetheless "of no great importance." It is superfluous, this questing—it is unnecessary. This sense of self-determination is what I believe Jane Bowles had in mind when she titled the novel—we are only truly serious when we're acting according to an *inner* prompting that has little or nothing to do with the world's pedestrian traffic and universal laws. It is only our *own* laws that we take seriously.

Two Serious Ladies is one of those works of art that acts on a reader's psyche in a subtle way that is hard to describe or appreciate fully; it represents a moral stance toward the world. The "argument" of the novel is impossible to paraphrase or summarize; it's a way of using language for a kind of meta-psychotherapeutic effect, a way of fending off anxiety by using words to render mental states "interesting" or "amusing" or surprisingly strange, but within the atmosphere of safety that is fostered by the linguistic play—the language is always playful and inventive, never forced or harsh. Most people find it a comfort to read a good novel, partly because the energy that comes from particularly expressive syntax gives us the feeling, which is not an illusion, that the writer is a kind of authority, and we're in good, capable hands.

Another of the pleasures associated with a writer as unpredictable and as honest as Jane Bowles is that of witnessing an act of uncovering or "coming clean." It was in her novel that the twenty-four-year-old Jane Bowles gave the fullest and most commanding account of her sexual feelings and her precocious audacity. Mrs. Copperfield, in

Panama City, is completely, madly in love with Pacifica, and in love with the girl's entire milieu, and she longs for nothing more. "Mrs. Copperfield's sole object in life was to be happy, although people who had observed her behavior over a period of years would have been surprised to discover that this was all." When she finds Pacifica hanging out at the Hotel de las Palmas, like Jane Bowles discovering lesbian society in Paris, perhaps, there is the shock of recognition, and the wish to hold on to something that is inevitably and obviously to be short-lived. During a walk around the city of Panama, Mrs. Copperfield has time to ask herself what she's doing, and what she wants to do. She "likes" her husband "above all other people," but her time with Pacifica and the proprietress of the hotel, Mrs. Quill, has given her an intensity of feeling that is completely new for her. "She began to feel a little exalted. There was a strong wind, and some lovely sailboats were passing by very swiftly not far from the shore. She threw her head back and closed her eyes, hoping that perhaps she might become exalted enough to run down and join her husband. But the wind did not blow quite hard enough, and behind her closed eyes she saw Pacifica and Mrs. Quill standing in front of the Hotel de las Palmas." She didn't feel "exalted enough" to return to her husband; just exalted enough to stay with her feelings about those captivating women for just a while longer.

GORE VIDAL'S 1948 NOVEL *The City and the Pillar* was the first novel by an American writer that sought to come fully and openly to terms with homosexuality as a viable, necessary, acceptable if inherently difficult way of life even for people who happen not to be freakish, effeminate, or suicidal. It is, as Michael Warner puts it, a gay novel "of the no-fats-or-femmes variety." It was also a popular bestseller and brought the subject of homosexuality, along with its author, permanently out of the closet.

In his 1995 memoir, *Palimpsest*, Vidal tells the real-life story that inspired the tragic love of one guy for another in *The City and the Pillar*. At a Washington DC boarding school, the very young Gore Vidal met a beautiful boy named Jimmie Trimble and they became intimate friends. They were roughly the same age, height, and weight, both blond. "His sweat," according to Vidal some fifty years later, "smelled of honey, like that of Alexander the Great." Jimmie was an athlete; he was perfection itself; he died—what could be more suggestive of perfection than this?—aged nineteen on Iwo Jima. The boys went to a DC theater to hear jazz together, they showered together after playing tennis, and they sometimes fooled around with each other in a sexual way. For Vidal, Jimmie was his "twin," his other half—the person that made him miraculously complete, satisfied, and happy. For Jimmie, however, Vidal was apparently just a friend. Jimmie may have been molested by his stepfather—he was sent to boarding school partly because, as his mother told Vidal much later, the German stepfather, "a fine decorator, a great horseman,"

liked Jimmie "altogether too much." But Jimmie was not gay, and his letters home during the war were to his mother and his girlfriend. He asked for a copy of *Leaves of Grass*, but no one knows what he thought of Whitman's homo-suggestive poems if he read them. The last time Vidal saw Jimmie was at a formal dance during the Christmas holiday of 1942, when they were seventeen.

In *The City and the Pillar*, Jim Willard, the protagonist, is obsessed with his friend Bob Ford, an athletic beauty with whom Jim shares an afternoon of sweet sexual experimentation one early summer day just after Bob has graduated high school. Bob leaves town shortly thereafter, and Jim is unable to keep track of his whereabouts. But the sexual experience with Bob was, for Jim, indelible, unforgettable, and transforming—it becomes the basis for Jim's whole conception of his sexuality. Jim compares all his later sexual experiences with that magical afternoon with Bob, and none of it is as good—nothing could be better, and in the end no one can embody Jim's ideal lover. Not even Bob can, when they meet again at the end of the story, since he's straight and interested only in his new wife. It's a fine mess Jim finds himself in. Not completely unlike the situation Gore Vidal himself is in as he writes about Jimmie Trimble in a memoir toward the end of his sixth decade—he reports that he has lived with a man for many years, but they have never enjoyed a sex life together and, besides, Vidal only likes to receive blow jobs, a strangely intimate assertion he reminds us of several times in *Palimpsest*. And nowadays he even prefers, he says, in order to keep things perfectly simple, to *pay* for those, "thus relieving" himself "of having to please anyone in any way."

The City and the Pillar and *Palimpsest* are both products of American gay culture in the sense that they were written at least partly in response to attitudes and beliefs about homosexuality that held gay people in contempt. Vidal was determined to show in each book that a gay person could be as "normal" as the rather uninteresting Jim Willard or the completely uningratiating, mature Gore Vidal. Jim's obsessive love for Bob—and Vidal's for Jimmie Trimble—is every bit as romantic and flawed as the love between any straight couple, and no more perverse or deranged. It's true that Jim ends up either killing Bob (in the original 1948 ending) or raping him and shattering the illusion of a happy ending to his protracted dream of love (in the much better revised version of 1965). But there is nothing about Jim's obsession with Bob that is particularly weird or decadent—it is "pure" longing, and more than lust. Jim doesn't want merely to have sex again with Bob; he wants them to be together permanently and intimately. The same is true of Vidal's longing feelings for the real-life though long-dead Jimmie Trimble.

Toward the end of *Palimpsest*, a book that is far stranger and more psychologically revealing and interesting than any of Vidal's novels including his best, *Myra Breckinridge*, the author tells us that he has met the woman, Chris White, who was once upon a time Jimmie Trimble's girlfriend. She tells him the story of another young man who'd been close to Jimmie, a frat boy called Carter. Shortly after Jimmie's death during the war: "All of a sudden Carter's fraternity brother came down out of the house and said, 'Something happened to Carter . . . he's been lying in his bed for three days and hasn't moved.' So he had to be removed from college. They diagnosed it as acute depression." Was Carter in love with Jimmie, too? In any case he eventually recovered and married. But Vidal wonders about their relationship, and he wonders a great deal about Jimmie, who never lived to see anything like gay liberation. Would he have been interested? "Jimmie was both homoerotic and heteroerotic. I suppose I am curious about the balance between the two in his nature. But then when one lover goes into shock at the news of his death and another mourns him to the end of his life, we have moved far beyond sex or eroticism and on to the wilder shores of love, and shipwreck." If the main theme of *Palimpsest* is Vidal's shipwreck upon the wilder shores of love, the primary subtext is that this early heartbreak provides the author with an excuse for being so thoroughly removed from the intimacy most people seek and give as they pass from adolescence to being an adult.

Palimpsest is also the writer's manifesto about how easy it is (even if you're gay) to become rich and successful by working hard at what one has a gift for doing—if you happen to know the right people, were born into the right family, and have the good luck to get a superior education. At the opening of the book, he quotes himself as having told a television interviewer that he "had never wanted to meet most of the people" he had met and that the fact that he "never got to know most of them took dedication and steadfastness." After all, if "you have known one person," Vidal proclaims, "you have known them all."

One thing Vidal does without fail—he tells what he considers to be the inescapable, ugly truth. He could look up to and feel proud of his father, but hated his mother, and he doesn't mind saying so. She had, according to Vidal, too many problems of her own. She does seem, in Vidal's ruthless description of her, a mean and sloppy alcoholic, concerned mostly about money and her image in the world; but she must have had *some* admirable qualities. Anyway, why linger over such an appalling state of affairs? It's bemusing, to say the least.

Though Vidal reports at length that he has always been attracted sexually *much* more to men than to women, he does not consider himself a homosexual—and he hates the idea of being so classified and labeled. He admits that he was often promiscuous in his pursuit and enjoyment of sex with men, mostly strangers. When he met the dancer Harold Lang, there seems to have been a moment in Vidal's life when he *almost* fell in love again—he fell briefly under the seductive belief that Lang was "Jimmie come back again." But it didn't take long for Vidal to realize that Harold Lang was not Jimmie

Trimble; and since he couldn't bring himself to be in love with any-one else, he gave the whole thing up—or Lang did. In any case, the affair did not last. "But during our short time together I was obliged to face the fact that I was never going to make the journey from homoerotic to homosexual and so I was never going to be able to have anything other than one-sided passing sex. Thanks to Harold, this belated revelation was to prove a great time-saver over the years." He was free, then, to accept his neatly paid-for blow jobs without getting involved in any messy, encumbering situations involving feelings or love or any of the other miserable trappings of homosexuality, which are aspects, of course, for most people, of being a person among other persons, and not at all tied to a specific sexuality.

Vidal apparently believed that "the fag world," which is made up of "grand queens" who hang around "faggot bars," would dislike *The City and the Pillar* not only because of its "lack of chic, but because the 'hetero' boy gets fucked by the protagonist." But as it turns out, many of the queens and faggots that have read the novel sometime during the fifty-odd years since its appearance, and have read Vidal's other books, too, *have* liked them, and have admired Vidal as a writer despite his hatred for himself and others. As a public intellectual and essayist, too, apart from his work as a novelist, Vidal is among our most valuable and exciting critics.

In his memoir, Vidal quotes the writer John Jay Chapman: "The thing that stirs us in any man's writing is the man himself—a thing quite outside the page, and for which the man is not responsible." In Vidal's case, I believe, we find an exception to that otherwise often true idea; I'm sometimes stirred by Vidal's writing, but never by the man, and that he is quite outside the page is what makes it possible to read his books with pleasure.

The First Time I Met Frank O'Hara

Vidal in his memoir reminds me of a few of the clients I encountered in the years I spent working as a prostitute in New York City during the late 1990s. Rich and untouchable, these geriatric gentlemen seemed bent on proving to me that, try as I might, there was simply no way to bring them anything more than mild, passing pleasure of the most superficial and trivial sort. Which was fine with me—I was just there for the money. But then, of course, one is never anywhere just for the money. As a matter of fact it did matter to me that these buttoned-down, straight-laced, nervous men could not be seduced into having a really worthwhile orgasm. They couldn't let me do my job well with them, and I always went away from that kind of a man feeling a little worse about both myself and other people. As if I'd brushed up against some sticky object that left a permanent, metallic smell and a small, faint abrasion on my skin. Rub as I might, the smell, and the little red scar, would never quite go away.

THE CITY AND THE PILLAR, curiously enough, probably could not have met with such widespread acclaim had Vidal sought to publish it even a few years later. At almost precisely the midpoint of the century, American culture was beclouded by a dark conservatism; it was a particularly hard time to be a young writer who was black, gay, and poor. James Baldwin's (1924-1987) second and best novel, *Giovanni's Room*, was rejected by Knopf, the publisher of his first (*Go Tell It on the Mountain,* 1953) in the mid-1950s because the publisher was afraid of legal action over the homosexual material around which the intimate story erotically circumnavigates. While this decision may not reflect well on the moral courage of Knopf at the time, it can also remind us of just how different the world was, even in New York City, a mere half century ago. Baldwin's agent advised him to burn the manuscript of *Giovanni's Room.* The novel, nevertheless, was published first in England and then, in 1956, by the Dial Press in New York without any legal incident. But there was in the air at the time a general and understandable wariness, a foreboding of repercussion and danger when the subject of homosexuality was broached in a less than condemnatory spirit. The first readers of Baldwin's new novel believed that its publication would be the end of his career and not—as in fact it turned out to be—the making of it.

America in the 1950s was, publicly and politically at least, a nightmare for the gay men and lesbians who chose, as Baldwin did, not to be completely closeted. Wisconsin Senator Joseph McCarthy (who, historians have hinted, may have been, as his powerful cohorts J. Edgar Hoover and Roy Cohn may have been, secretly bisexual or gay) was an outspoken, highly visible model of hateful homophobia. As Charles Kaiser reports in *The Gay Metropolis: 1940–1996*, McCarthy once told a group of reporters that to be "against McCarthy, boys, you've got to be a communist or a cocksucker." Under his influence, President Eisenhower signed an order in 1953 that listed "sexual perversion" as "sufficient and necessary ground for disbarment from federal jobs." According to Kaiser, "During the next sixteen months, at least 640 homosexuals were removed from government employment. That number probably understates the real figure because many were allowed to resign without being forced to disclose their sexuality." Baldwin never worked for the government, but he was a public figure in the 1950s (and a "well-known pervert"), and the FBI kept a close eye on him for many years. His file there eventually added up to 1,302 pages.

Giovanni's Room was by far the most homoerotic of novels yet to be brought before the American public. Set in Paris—that sexiest of cities, at least in the American imagination—the consummated passion of young American David for beautiful Italian Giovanni was a true case of *coup de foudre*, of lust verging on love. Giovanni takes lovemaking to be the most serious of all human pursuits, and his affair with David, once in full swing, is, for him, of the utmost importance for the sustenance and health of his mind and his fiery Latin soul (and the end of their affair is followed quickly by the end of Giovanni, who is executed after being convicted of murder). There may be little explicit description of sex between David and Giovanni; but it's very clear that they had sex with each other over and over again for months while they lived together in Giovanni's bohemian little

apartment, and it's very clear from Baldwin's writing that the two characters both enjoyed it, to put it mildly. The sex David has with Giovanni, in fact—or to be more romantic about it, the relationship they have with each other—spoils David for the respectable heterosexual life he was intending (and resumes trying, for a while) to have with Hella, his perfectly intelligent and likeable and attractive girlfriend. David ends up with neither Giovanni nor Hella; but if he ends up with a sexual identity, it's a good deal more gay than straight. He doesn't suffer from losing Hella the way he suffers from losing Gio-vanni—*she* hasn't the power over him to destroy his peace of mind, though she'd like to by the end of their affair.

David's story is that of a young gay man going through the bitter, confusing heartbreak that comes, as it does for many people, with gradual, reluctant, uneasy acceptance of being gay. As Sigmund Freud wrote in a 1935 letter to the mother of a young American gay man (and unwilling, unhappy gay people would roundly confirm), "Homosexuality is assuredly no advantage...." (Freud finished his thought, though, with the following: "...but it is nothing to be ashamed of, no vice, no degradation, it cannot be classified as an ill-ness....") David is disappointed that life has turned out for him to be different and more complex than he would like it to be. A part of him, at least, would be content with a middle-class heterosexual life of marriage, work, parenthood, and monogamy; but not the bigger part of him. He can't help being gay, as few if any of us can, and aside from some ecstatic moments with Giovanni, the David of Baldwin's novel has not found a way to enjoy or appreciate being gay. He does, how-ever, find a way to enjoy sex with Giovanni.

In the criticism I've seen about *Giovanni's Room*, surprisingly little attention has been given to the sexual activity alluded to in the novel, probably because Baldwin was not more explicit about it. But I believe his reticence is erotic in itself, and that his great novel is bor-derline pornographic. The definition of pornography, after all, emphasizes the intention to arouse, and does not refer exclusively to material in which sex is described or portrayed. I believe Baldwin did intend to arouse his readers, partly as a political act: leading readers along the garden path toward gay sex was one way to subvert the dominant (straight) sexual ethos of the 1950s. And Baldwin was nothing if not a troublemaker when it came to sexual and racial politics. During the '60s, Baldwin was known to disillusion liberal white people by answering their queries about the intentions of black activists by saying, "Yes, baby, they're going to burn your house down."

The sexual tension in *Giovanni's Room* begins to build very early on, when David recalls a teenage sexual romp with Joey, "a very nice boy . . . very quick and dark, and always laughing." Joey was, "for a while," David's best friend. One night after a long day together, the two boys are in bed when Joey wakes up from a dream. David teases him and tells him to go back to sleep; they laugh and begin wrestling around on the bed, as they had done plenty of times, innocently enough, before. David grabbed Joey's head, just as he had done in the past. "But this time," David recalls, "when I touched him something happened in him and in me which made this touch different from any touch either of us had ever known." Things proceed as things sometimes do when two teenage boys are in bed together. "Joey raised his head as I lowered mine and we kissed, as it were, by accident. Then, for the first time in my life, I was really aware of another person's body, of another person's smell. . . . I was very frightened; I am sure he was frightened too, and we shut our eyes." What happened next is left for us to imagine.

David ends his friendship with Joey by treating him very badly. He's driven by shame and fear to denounce the boy and to lie to him, eventually, about dating a girl; David joins a "rougher, older crowd." He was "very nasty to Joey. And the sadder this made him the nastier [he] became."

When the novel opens, years have passed, and David is involved with Hella, but she is traveling in Spain, and David is left to his own devices in Paris. Someone he knows, Jacques, who happens to be rich and gay, introduces David to a bar owned by Guillaume, the man Giovanni will end up being accused of killing. It's in this bar that David first meets Giovanni, who's working as barman. David, like just about everyone else, is immediately attracted and enchanted by Giovanni, who is not only beautiful to look at, but smart and sharp and selective with his affections. When the guy everyone else wants wants David, the American can do nothing but submit. In fact, he falls in love. "I think we connected the instant that we met," David narrates. "Until I die there will be those moments, moments seeming to rise up out of the ground like Macbeth's witches, when his face will come before me, that face in all its changes, when the exact timbre of his voice and tricks of his speech will nearly burst my ears, when his smell will overpower my nostrils."

Jacques, despite more than a pang of jealousy, and after a long night of drinking steadily, encourages David to seize the day, or the night. "'*Somebody,*' said Jacques, 'your father or mine, should have told us that not many people have ever died of love. But multitudes have perished, and are perishing every hour—and in the oddest places!—for the lack of it.' And then: 'Here comes your baby. *Sois sage. Sois chic.*'" And early that first morning, David found himself surprisingly hooked. "And here my baby came indeed, through all that sunlight, his face flushed and his hair flying, his eyes, unbelievably, like morning stars." The two go to Giovanni's room that morning for the first time; and David is ravished.

> He locked the door behind us, and then for a moment, in the
> gloom, we simply stared at each other—with dismay, with relief,
> and breathing hard. I was trembling. I thought, if I do not open
> the door at once and get out of here, I am lost. But I knew I could

not open the door, I knew it was too late; soon it was too late to do anything but moan. He pulled me against him, putting himself into my arms as though he were giving me himself to carry, and slowly pulled me down with him to that bed. With everything in me screaming *No!* yet the sum of me sighed *Yes.*

This portrayal of two young men about to make love with each other was, in the mid-1950s, an astonishingly brazen, and brave, act of social effrontery. This is one of those clear-cut cases of an artist getting away with an almost criminal act of taboo-breaking by placing that act within a great work of art. I'm not suggesting that Baldwin would have been arrested for writing a bad novel loaded with gay sex; but a bad novel would not have put a gay love story so memorably into the popular imagination the way *Giovanni's Room* did. The story of David and Giovanni is important in terms of literary *and* social history because the novel in which that story is told is such a persuasive work of art.

Giovanni's Room is, among other things, a triumph of gay culture. In one of the earliest of his many great essays, "Everybody's Protest Novel" (published in *Zero*, a magazine, in 1949 and reprinted since in *Notes of a Native Son*), Baldwin attacked the kind of literary work that aimed merely to argue a political point from the position of powerlessness and weakness, of "protest" rather than persuasion. For a novel, according to Baldwin, to have a lasting and transforming effect, it would have to do justice to the fullness and complexity of human beings as portrayed in narrative prose; it would need to accept life as it really is, with all of life's real and particular quandaries, obscurities, and pleasures. "The failure of the protest novel lies in its rejection of life, the human being, the denial of his beauty, dread, power, in its insistence that it is his categorization alone which is real and which cannot be transcended." Baldwin dreamed of—and then accomplished with *Giovanni's Room*—a kind of literary art that was in itself an act of protest; in which the writing *is* the argument; and in which the argument is the self-evident claim that telling the truth—the whole truth—in detail and without sentimentality—is what an artist does.

I HAD A POET FOR A BOYFRIEND for about a year shortly after I moved to New York in 1988; he died of AIDS in the early '90s. Gerard lived on Staten Island—he liked it there—he liked the quiet and the distance from the city, and I traveled on many a cold, quiet evening from Manhattan to the house Gerard shared with some friends about a mile's walk inland, most of it up an icy hill. Those long trips on my way to see him became an integral part of my experience with Gerard, since his poetry, and that of the poets he admired and talked to me about, was composed partly in response to some of the very elements I encountered on my journeying to and from Staten Island on the ferry: stretches of solitary time, the changing qualities of the light and the weather, the sea, and the pleasures of the senses in general. The peak of my relationship with Gerard, when I went to see him most often, was wintertime, and that, too, seemed to be reflected in the poetry he would show me, his own and that of poets like his teacher Bernadette Mayer and his heroes, the New York School poets. I remember sitting at a little round table in a café in Greenwich Village with Gerard as he read aloud to me the closing pages of Mayer's *Midwinter's Day*. The poetry itself, and Gerard's reading of it to me in that café, took me by surprise, as I believe my reaction to it (I shed a tear or two) surprised Gerard; he seemed moved to have found a friend, a lover, as susceptible to the sometimes almost painful beauty of poetry as he was. It was a moment, for me, memorably laden with an intense and astonishing feeling.

I was totally unprepared for Gerard's death a few years after we

split up, but I had the good fortune to be present for his last months, and his was the most chillingly sublime death I've known firsthand. He died, so to speak, with poetry on his lips. So it should come as no surprise, I guess, that much of the poetry he taught me to love, which on the one hand is so full of life and energy, has always been tinged, in my mind, with the cold outside as well as the warmth within; with decay; and with a sense of hibernation and withdrawal.

Apart from work by Gerard's friends and his own poetry, the

poems he liked best when I knew him were by the so-called New York School poets—John Ashbery, Kenneth Koch, James Schuyler, and especially Frank O'Hara. The kind of lyrics by these poets that Gerard loved most were based on quiet and playful indoor observation by the poet of another person who might be asleep or silently occupied with a book or work; these poems begin with the minute and particular and usually end up commenting subtly on some bigger aspect of life. Here's a good example by Schuyler, called "Watching You":

> Watching you sleep
> a thing you do so well
> no shove no push
> on the sliding face
> of sleep as on
> the deep a sea bird
> of a grand wingspread
> trusts what it knows
> and I who rumple crumple
> and mash (snore) amble
> and ankle about wide
> awake, wanting to fold,
> loving to watch sleep
> embodied in you my
> warm machine that draws
> me back to bed
> and you who turn
> all toward me
> to love and seduce
> me back to sleep "You

said 9:30, now it's
10:" you
don't seem to care
cold coffee (sugar,
no milk) about time:
you never do, never
get roiled the way
I do "Should I nag
you or shut up? If
you say, I will"
always be
glad to return to
that warming turning
to me in that
tenderest moment
of my nights,
and more, my days.

For me, there is nothing more romantic than a poem like "Watching You" that has come to be associated in some intimate, unique way with a person I've known well and loved, even if imperfectly and inadequately, as I loved the poet Gerard Rizza. Schuyler, like the poets and painters that were his closest friends, was sensitive to aspects of the world that are easily overlooked and often quickly forgotten—the elusive "tenderest moment" of the day or night. As another great poet, Douglas Crase, once wrote about this quality in Schuyler's poetry, "We call it the everyday, when it is more likely that experience is the one thing that is not commonplace, the one source of the saving distinctions that give us lives."

Gerard was sensitive in that way, too, and his own poetry gives a clear reflection of his subtle preoccupations. His poems were collected in a small volume called *Regard for Junction* published in an edition of five hundred copies by an outfit with a name I always thought cruelly macabre, given Gerard's losing battle with AIDS (though the name gave Gerard himself intense pleasure): Spectacular Diseases, from England. Inserted into the copy I have is a white card with a gloomy black border that reads, on the front side:

i.m.

Gerard Rizza

1959–1992

And on the back: "Because of Gerard Rizza's death on the 4th April 1992, there is no signed edition of this book." The thirty-five poems inside, which are among the few traces of my friend that I have, are not inferior, in my mind, to the poems he liked by better-known and longer-surviving poets like Schuyler and Ashbery (O'Hara, like Gerard, died young, though not as young as Gerard—he lived to be forty, Gerard just thirty-three). Here, from Gerard's only book, is the poem that closes it, "As I Lay Winking," which he wrote in my bedroom in Brooklyn one night while I was asleep.

> Books change since I was last here.
> Green crane from a glance at staves.
> Boots piled and the Chinese slippers back from my place.
> Unfolded and framed sister's drawing.
> Read your cards, throw your coins,
> help yourself to your life, young.

The First Time I Met Frank O'Hara

> I didn't mean to stay,
> just came to apologize
> for projecting the whole book of my dead
> onto your leaving.
> Do you be.
> Translate a controversy of remembering.
> A black zip bead.

There's a refreshing lack of grandiosity about the poems by Gerard and the New York School poets, a seeming offhandedness and an unpretentiousness that gives the best of their work an impressive quality of just having been improvised by an eccentric, fanciful genius. Much of their work is, in the best sense, light and spacious, which is not to suggest that these poets fail to meet whatever darkness or complexity attends their thoughts (and for Ashbery—he is the only one of the four major New York School poets still living—there seems always to be as much complexity as clarity, and as much darkness as light). It seems, somehow, pertinent and interesting that three of the four major poets of the New York School (Ashbery, Schuyler, and O'Hara) were gay. Even Koch, who was not, "talked and acted," according to his friend Larry Rivers, "as gay as the rest." In *The Last Avant-Garde: The Making of the New York School of Poets*, David Lehman writes about the poetics of the group, which could also, coincidentally, be read as a general description of at least one type of literary gay sensibility: "They felt that the value of a poem rested not in the nobility of the sentiment behind it but in the pleasure it gave to the reader. Agreeing with Oscar Wilde that 'All bad poetry springs from genuine feeling,' they guarded vigilantly against sentimentality in their work.... Poetry did not have to be limited by

the life experience of the poet; it could be generated linguistically, conjured up via innovative methods of composition. Poetry was not life, but it did suggest—and embody—an aesthetic form of life, liberty, and the pursuit of happiness. And this pursuit was chronicled, explored, memorialized, and enacted in their poems."

An "aesthetic form of life" is a good way of referring to the way these poets sought to live and work. Their poems included all the aspects of their lives. John Ashbery's work, especially lately, is famously hard to make sense of, but on the other hand sense is not exactly what Ashbery purports to make. The condition of his mind and the tone of his emotional life—that is what his work conveys above all else. Ashbery almost always skips the storyline element that most poets use to ground the reader in a recognizable or easily hospitable atmosphere. "I find," he once told an interviewer, "one can say very much more by advancing immediately to the poetry in the poem."

<0>

If Gerard had been forced to choose one poet of all the ones he loved, he probably would have taken Frank O'Hara, the gay writer I most regret not having known personally. After he died in 1966, many of his close friends, mostly poets, painters, and composers, eventually wrote and published something about him. The first volume of memoirs was a dazzling collection of poems, essays, and pictures edited by Bill Berkson and Joe LeSueur in 1978, *Homage to Frank O'Hara.* In a short essay, O'Hara's friend Morton Feldman (a great American composer whose work O'Hara loved) wrote about the "immortal" pain left behind by an artist who dies young. "Looking at Mondrian's total output, we see a man who had completed a consummate journey. What regrets can we have? But do we ever hear a melody of Schubert's without that sense of a life cut short, of genius cut short?" O'Hara's *Collected Poems* is a hefty volume of more than five hundred pages; but the great poems would fill only a medium-sized book. Of those, it is impossible to read one without that feeling of a major artist having been snatched away from us prematurely. The best poems by O'Hara have a youthful quality that I love; but what might he have done if he'd lived to be fifty, or ninety?

O'Hara's most successful poems also have a lustfulness about them—a lust for life, for sensual intensity, for emotional stimulation and communication. O'Hara, who came of age during the McCarthy era, was completely open about his sexuality, and of all poets he may be the most ideally suited to represent an openly gay literary style. His poems (and his life) exude all the things I think of as characterizing a gay sensibility: incisive wit, reckless energy, irony, resourcefulness, ambition, tenderness, ambivalence, continual surprise. Here, in the opening of "Post the Lake Poets Ballad," from 1959, there is also the wonderful O'Hara trademark feeling of not suffering, at the moment, from any of the troubles or problems or anxiety that may lurk elsewhere in his mind:

> Moving slowly sweating a lot
> I am pushed by a gentle breeze
> outside the Paradise Bar on
> St. Marks Place and I breathe

A recent book by O'Hara's longtime friend, roommate, and sometime lover, Joe LeSueur, called *Digressions on Some Poems by Frank O'Hara,* gives a great deal of intimate, firsthand information about the poems O'Hara wrote while LeSueur lived with him in a series of New York apartments. They first met in 1951 at a concert; John Ashbery introduced them. Four years later LeSueur moved in to "Squalid Manor," O'Hara's apartment on East Forty-ninth Street (so named by their friend William Weaver), and they stuck together for ten years, which were, LeSueur implies, the most interesting and memorable ten years of his life—and of O'Hara's life, too. There was little jealousy in their home, even though O'Hara sometimes took over LeSueur's lovers and vice-versa. The roommates sometimes slept together, but not often after they'd been living together a while; they were close friends, and they supported each other and prevented each other from suffering much from loneliness. LeSueur recognized O'Hara's genius right away, and he surely fell somewhat in love with him, as many people did. O'Hara probably realized that in LeSueur he had found a loyal, reliable companion and confidant who was both readily available and not too demanding (LeSueur also shopped and cooked; O'Hara didn't). And LeSueur was extremely good-looking. Writing about the time when they began living together in the summer of 1955, LeSueur muses, "Did we know what we were getting into? I certainly didn't; only in hindsight have I been able to sort this out—even now, I'm not sure I have it right. It was all unspoken; we'd not yet had sex; and in the end, the ambiguous nature of our relationship would be our undoing." Neither of them managed to have something they both claimed to want, a monogamous long-term boyfriend, though they both had numerous affairs. And they finally split up, toward the end of 1964. "It was, of course, my attachment to Frank that ruled out my forming a lasting romantic relationship with any of my boyfriends—his presence in my life was that encompassing. Even as late as the spring and summer of 1964, only months before it was decided we could no longer be together, I found living under the same roof with him a solace and a pleasure, an *anchor*, in spite of our not being as close as we once were."

LeSueur's book is divided into chapters, each of which is headed by an O'Hara poem or an excerpt from one. Some of the poems refer directly to Joe LeSueur, some of them were written in LeSueur's presence, and all of them contain references LeSueur has special knowledge of since he was so closely involved in the poet's life at the time. For example, LeSueur tells us that O'Hara wrote the poem

"June 2, 1958" after having met Patsy Southgate, who had just started dating Mike Goldberg, O'Hara and LeSueur's good friend. Southgate would herself shortly be among O'Hara's closest friends. One sentence from the poem ("Meanwhile, / back at Patsy South-gate's, two grown men / are falling off a swing into a vat of Bloody Marys.") leads LeSueur to a theory about why the circle of friends was so mutually compatible and attractive. "Conjecture on my part, it goes like this: Patsy wouldn't have fallen in love with Mike, much less married him, if his rough manner and bravado had not been off-set by what his two gay friends embodied, a homosexuality that was gracefully assimilated into straight society without being closeted, a homosexuality that was carefree without being giddy, a homosexuality that was also gentle, amused, and ironic, and a homosexuality that embraced what so many gays as well as straight men abjure, the inner feminine part of the male personality. . . . a homosexuality whose pro-scription of misogyny Patsy could only have found novel and reassuring, a comfort and a boon. . . ."

O'Hara's most productive and happiest period was when he was in love with a handsome, very young dancer, Vincent Warren, who was also in love with him. (Warren was twenty when they met; O'Hara was thirty-three). The first of many poems O'Hara wrote while involved with Warren had the appealing title "You Are Gorgeous and I'm Coming." LeSueur says of Warren, "Yes, he was gorgeous, with thick eye-lashes, a perfect profile, a ballet dancer's great body—but there was a lot more to him than that." The poems from this period of O'Hara's short happy life are among the most infectiously cheerful, amusing, inventive lyrics by any serious American poet. One of the poems, for example, which O'Hara didn't bother to title (it's referred to as "Poem" and identified by its first line, "Khrushchev is coming on the

right day!") ends with: "and the light seems to be eternal / and joy seems to be inexorable / I am foolish enough always to find it in wind."

O'Hara's best poems seem to have been very easily composed, as if he had just casually jotted down his thoughts about the day and what was currently occupying his mind. The *poetry* in the poems is light, almost careless, as if O'Hara could count on his reader to find it with very little help from him. There is a kind of tacit assumption that the poem is really a poem—he doesn't have to prove it. O'Hara's freedom and talent as an artist, together with the emotional energy he apparently enjoyed on account of his romantic good fortune with Vincent Warren, combined to produce the circumstances in which the poet could write some of the most memorable love poems in our history. These poems never sink into sentimentality or silliness; they express a state of mind and an emotional condition that corresponds to one version of human aspiration fully realized and embodied and experienced. In the middle of the twentieth century, O'Hara's was (and perhaps still is) as sophisticated and complete as transcendence need be.

I GREW UP BELIEVING that the man whose name I bear was my father; but now he says he's not my father and—by some clever, manly logic—never was. He was certainly not a good parent, but at least he was, I thought, my dad. Another candidate, whose name my mother has lately recalled, is supposed to be someplace in Indiana with his own family, which was begun before I was (and which prevented him—the man my mother loved—from being her husband). These sad facts make some of James Purdy's best-known fiction of particular interest for me, since the myth of a loving and protective father—and his eternal absence—haunts much of his work, especially "63: Dream Palace" and *Malcolm*. Disappearing, according to Purdy, is what fathers do best. What sons mostly do, in turn, is wander the earth without rest or satisfaction.

The main characters of both these works are lost, amenable boys. Fenton Riddleway, the nineteen-year-old hero of the 1956 novella "63: Dream Palace" is a sort of ambivalent father figure to his younger brother, Claire. They are, apparently, fatherless—their father is barely mentioned in the story at all—and their mother recently died. They come from West Virginia and have landed in the unnamed city (which could be New York) on the suggestion of a mysterious friend, Kincaid, who told them about a house on "Sixty-three Street." The house is, for Fenton, "a not-right house." Besides being bug infested and possibly haunted, the problem with the house for Fenton is that there "ain't nobody in it for one thing. . . . I keep thinking how empty it is, and what are we waiting for after all. . . ." The "not-right house" isn't the only empty thing in Fenton's life; his is the story of a lonely orphan in the impossible position of premature responsibility for a younger sibling.

Fenton's much younger brother Claire is a helpless, ailing child who relies entirely on his brother to provide for him, to protect him, to keep him company, to love him. But Fenton, barely old enough to be considered an adult himself, is unprotected and uncared for, too, and eventually he caves in and, inevitably, breaks down. The love between the two boys, the intimacy between them, and Fenton's terrible indifference toward his brother, which he uses to defend himself emotionally, all contribute to the intense feeling of "63: Dream Palace," which may be Purdy's short-form masterpiece.

<⋄>

When we first meet fourteen-year-old Malcolm, the title character of Purdy's 1959 novel, he's sitting on a bench in front of a hotel being questioned by Mr. Cox, an astrologer he just met, who insists that Malcolm has "a *waiting* look." Malcolm at first denies that he's waiting for anyone, but "My father has disappeared," he admits, and he reluctantly confesses that "perhaps I may be waiting for him."

Later, he meets Kermit, a midget, who greets Malcolm by saying, "So you are the boy who is infatuated with his father." Malcolm doesn't realize or admit that he's infatuated with his missing father, but one of the things the people he meets find so attractive about the boy is the sweet expectancy and hopefulness he sustains with regard to his absent father. Malcolm never whines or complains— he waits. Some of the people he meets begin to wonder if Malcolm thinks about anything else, he seems so passively resigned to wait-

ing for his father. "Does Malcolm have any mind at all?" Kermit asks Mr. Cox. "Do you think he needs one?" the astrologer replies.

Everybody wants to be with Malcolm, but Malcolm's not sure where he wants to be if not on the bench outside the hotel waiting for his father. He leaves the bench only after Mr. Cox presents him with the first of a series of names and addresses. The experience he has of meeting the people Mr. Cox sends him to gives him the vague sense that his life is only now truly beginning—that waiting for his father was childish and should be given up. But putting his father behind him, Malcolm finds, is impossible. Everywhere he goes, his father is still not there. Having found himself in yet another strange house, Malcolm can hear music coming from upstairs, "the sad persistent notes of bass and sax, piano and vibraphone and drums..." He'd been told not to leave the room under any circumstances:

> Malcolm felt himself then entirely alone, more alone than had he remained on the bench. In the lonely emptiness of the house, with its castlelike high ceilings, the feel of the gray thick carpets beneath his feet, and the self-portraits of Eloisa, the drawings of Negroes looking out from their pales eyes, of strange perhaps nonexistent animals gazing at him from canvases everywhere, Malcolm remembered his early travels with his father in countries whose names he could no longer recall. But this time, he was more hopelessly alone, in addition to not understanding anything around him. And at the same time he rather felt that perhaps he belonged here as much as anywhere, with the colored musicians, the paintings, and the different bed each night.

I can't help but think, reading that forlorn paragraph, of fatherless gay young men, having found themselves, as I did once, in the big city that turns out, at least at first, to be a far lonelier and stranger place than they'd bargained for, wondering if they've done the right thing in going there at all. Malcolm is never sure that he shouldn't go back to the harmless bench and just keep on waiting for his father. The world away from the bench, though, is too fascinating; it's too much fun to be wanted, even if it's not his father that wants him. One of Malcolm's most ardent admirers, Madame Girard, tells her husband that she longs for "the sight of Malcolm, before whom I only wish to light candles. My loves have always been of that type. The candle-lighting type." Who could resist such esteem?

Malcolm's decision to give up waiting for his father on the bench changes his life drastically and in many ways. Madame Girard's husband, Girard Girard, who is wealthy and also loves Malcolm, wishes to leave his wife, marry another woman (Kermit the midget's wife) and take Malcolm away to live in the country, where Malcolm could have whatever he wanted. "'But I had everything until just a few days ago,' the boy cried. 'And suddenly, having left the bench entirely . . . for reasons I do not recall—I have *nothing*.'" Girard Girard assures Malcolm that the boy has *him*. "'I have lost everything!' the boy said, and then his violence disintegrated into a sudden calm and even sweetness." He doesn't want to go away to the countryside with Girard because he doesn't want to miss out on anything in town. "'You can't go on by yourself!'" Girard tells him. "'But what if Mr. Cox should give me more addresses!'" Malcolm cries. He's turned promiscuous despite himself.

Lots of things happen to Malcolm—he gets tattooed, he gets married, he accosts a man that he mistakes for his father in a bathroom and is taken away by the police. Malcolm's new wife, a young, very famous singer called Melba, can't figure out why her young husband should want to find his father anyway. After his arrest, she tries to rid him of his "*idée* unfix": "'Who wants a father?'" she asks him. "'It's been old hat for years.'" Malcolm insists that the man in the bathroom looked just like his father. "'Millions of men look like millions of men, especially Americans,' Melba said, beginning on a new drink the waiter had just brought her. 'In fact, most men look like most men. That's why I go for you, kiddy. You're unique all over.'"

Eventually a doctor is called in to see what's the matter with poor Malcolm, who appears to be ill. "The physician, a man, who, as Melba noted immediately, looked fatally ill himself, gave this diagnosis: Malcolm was dying, he claimed, from acute alcoholism and sexual hyperaesthesia, and all that could be done for him now was give him every comfort and a quiet bed to himself."

‹◊›

Malcolm is the kind of young man one doesn't really want to know in life. He may be engaging and lively and he is surely beautiful. But the Malcolm type is on a mission that blinds him to the value of other people—he's essentially a troublemaker, though he doesn't mean to be. He's an innocent criminal. What the world has to offer, for every Malcolm, is not what he is looking for.

He may manage to grow up and may even become an adult; or he may not. He may be a good fuck when he's young, but he can't be a good lover. He has to find a way, somehow, to stop needing his father's protection and stop wanting his father's love, which he'll never have. . . .

STEVEN MOORE, writing in the *Washington Post*, compared Andrew Holleran's 1996 novel *The Beauty of Men* with F. Scott Fitzgerald's *The Great Gatsby*. As Fitzgerald had done in the '20s, Moore says, Holleran "eulogizes his generation's experiences in a sensuous, elegant style." I find the comparison of the two novelists even more apt in connection with Holleran's earlier novel, his 1978 *Dancer from the Dance*. Both *Gatsby* and *Dancer* feature charming, brilliant narrators who witness high-stakes goings-on involving some rich and alluring characters, and in both novels the shenanigans end disastrously, with death and, to put it simply, loss of innocence.

In both *The Great Gatsby* and *Dancer from the Dance*, the narrators have a wonderful wry sensibility that gives their observation and depiction of the action a kind of generous, concerned, but somewhat detached and weary character. When Nick Carraway visits his friends Daisy and Tom Buchanan near the beginning of *Gatsby*, he gets his first look at Jordan Baker, the woman he falls "half in love" with. He finds Daisy and Jordan "buoyed up" on an enormous sofa in the Buchanans' large living room. "The younger of the two was a stranger to me. She was extended full length at her end of the divan, completely motionless and with her chin raised a little as if she were balancing something on it which was quite likely to fall. If she saw me out of the corner of her eyes she gave no hint of it—indeed I was almost surprised into murmuring an apology for having disturbed her by coming in." So polite, while at the same time so intelligent and rigorous and fair.

The unnamed narrator of Holleran's novel is almost a gay version of Nick Carraway, in the late 1970s rather than the early 1920s. Here the narrator watches Malone, the object of so much desire in this lusty novel, as he enters a nightclub where he's well-known and well liked. Malone is immediately surrounded by other handsome young men, a few of his many acquaintances: "He put an arm around their shoulders or shook their hands, with his almost old-fashioned manners. He put his head close to theirs when they spoke to him, as if he didn't want to miss a word, and when he replied he spoke almost against their ear: a charming gesture ostensibly to defeat the noise of the room, but one that made you feel you were being winnowed out, selected, for some confidential revelation."

Dancer From the Dance opens and closes with a few letters back and forth between the author of the long middle-section manuscript (which is the bulk of the novel) and a friend who has moved away from New York (and would *"rather die like a beast in the fields . . . than go back"*) and lives now in the "Deep South." These letters are meant to set up and then briefly comment upon the novel itself; but the letters themselves are miniature masterpieces of late-period, full-on gay culture, an example of a subculture having opened up a new means of expression (it supplied, so to speak, the conditions in which Holleran could do his work). The first letter is from the friend down south, and the first lines seem strangely prescient and foreboding, coming as they do from the relatively happy days of the 1970s, when just about everything sexually transmittable could be cured with penicillin. *"It's finally spring down here on the Chatta-hoochee—the azaleas are in bloom, and everyone is dying of cancer. I am writing you very late at night."* Very late, indeed, given that AIDS would within a matter of a few years kill most of

The First Time I Met Frank O'Hara

Andrew Holleran's friends, which we know from his shattering 1988 book of essays, *Ground Zero*. As Ernie McLeod has written, "Though *Dancer* was written and set in the 70's, it has a haunted, elegiac quality that seems to foreshadow the AIDS epidemic, adding an eerie bite to its pathos and humor."

Dancer from the Dance, more than any other novel, gives a reader such as myself, who missed the '70s (I was a child at the time), some idea of what it was like in New York City after Stonewall and before AIDS: the Golden Age of Homosexuality, I suppose. It must have been exhausting as well as exhilarating to be a part of what Holleran refers to as the milieu of the Great Queens, ". . . the true loonies of this society, refusing to camouflage themselves for society's sake." The guys in *Dancer* take their pleasure seriously. They arrange their lives so that nothing can stop them from going out at night or from getting to Fire Island in summertime. Making his way to the Pines at the beginning of a new season, Malone, the beautiful star of the story, passes through a quaint little town on Long Island that strikes him as the perfect place for another kind of person to spend the summer; but not for him or those like him who were "so bent on pleasure they were driving right through Happiness, it seemed, a quieter brand of existence that flourished under these green elms." Malone and his friends "kept driving right through all the dappled domesticity, like prisoners, indeed, being moved from jail to jail imprisoned in our own sophistication."

The will to have fun at any cost is a personality trait many of us learn from our parents—like them, we find ourselves one day to be adults who don't want to miss anything while we're still young. The drudgery of trying hard to have fun is one of the contradictory themes of Holleran's story. Just as one can't separate the dancer from the dance, for Malone and his friends there is finally no distinction between their homosexuality and a kind of decadence. They go to so much trouble looking for fun that they seldom have a very good time, and even when they are having fun, they always see something else coming up—something dark and final. So they do what we all do: they postpone and defer and distract themselves—by trying to have fun. Fun and the end of fun: in the lives of people lucky enough to have the time and resources and an unworried enough state of mind, that is one of the recurring cycles we live with, like companionship and loneliness. If the fun never ends, it never started; if we're never lonely, then we never really had a friend.

‹◇›

There was another important gay novel published in the same year, 1978. Larry Kramer's scathing *Faggots*, published (astonishingly, given its outlandish raunchiness) by Random House, was clearly meant to shock. On the third page we find Fred Lemish in a bathhouse trying to decide whether or not he should have sex with two guys he thinks of as master and slave, though they both seem perfectly willing to change roles at the drop of a towel. First Fred is asked by the master to piss on them, then to be pissed on by them. "Or fuck my friend and I'll suck your come out of his asshole." This must have been among the first and only overt references to "filching" in the mainstream media of the 1970s. "Are you into shit?" Fred is asked, and after only the slightest hesitation, he goes ahead and fucks the slave, an experience he finds neither wholly satisfying nor particularly regrettable, which is pretty much his attitude toward his life generally.

Lemish, just one of the many self-loathing faggots in Kramer's novel, is an aspiring writer, good-looking, neurotic, promiscuous, selfish. He broods at length on two subjects that seem somehow linked together for him: Dinky (the guy he desires) and his own bowel movements. His nervousness about Dinky affects his entire life (and his grammar): "... he was scared shitless, or perhaps this is better phrased as scared into shitlessness, was this actually happening to him: *Love?!*"

I think of *Faggots* (which was reissued in 2000 in an attractive new edition) as one of the necessary productions of a time in which there was a kind of cultural pressure on gay men to do *something* by way of leaving a lasting, appropriate record of what was going on in big cities like New York. Gay men were liberated, intelligent, talented, and living unprecedentedly open gay lives, and some of them were having a great time. The ensuing complications of this sometimes hedonistic, relatively carefree lifestyle—even aside from the eventual tragedy that could not have been fully foreseen even by the most pessimistic prophet—were beyond rich with suggestiveness about human nature. It was an unusual time in which a lot of gay men had the wherewithal to do exactly what they thought they wanted to do, on their own terms, with nothing holding them back. Their lives seemed to be, for a while, their own. Someone had to write a novel about it; Kramer, who was a playwright and screenwriter, obliged with *Faggots*.

<‹›>

While Holleran's 1978 novel makes use of milder material to portray its version of the gay underworld at the time, *Dancer from the Dance* is, for me, as flawless and as impressive as *The Great Gatsby*. It's not shocking the way *Faggots* is (and there is something to be said for being shocking), but *Dancer* is a powerful piece of work that's shown no sign of fading. Considered by many to be *the* gay novel of the post-Stonewall decade, *Dancer from the Dance* lives on in a way that dance clubs and denizens of the night like those that inhabit the story also live on, with a certain admirable energy that seems to be—and I hope it is—inexhaustible.

WHEN DAVID WOJNAROWICZ (1955-1992) was seventeen, before he became famous as a downtown NYC painter, writer, photographer, ex-hustler, and AIDS activist, he made some entries in a diary while he was on an Outward Bound trip to Hurricane Island. These entries are the beginning of what was published in 1999 as *In the Shadow of the American Dream*, a remarkable selection from his journals:

> Thursday, August 9, 1971
> The first day we were coming over by ferry. It was foggy and the mist whipped at our faces. I was cold as hell. I started talking to my friend next to me whom I met at the airport. Soon he left with his friend and I sat behind a car to keep out of the cold. I began a conversation with a boy who was to be in my watch; his name was Tony. He is from Long Island.

This is slightly awkward, precocious, very loveable adolescent writing; in it are a few of the methods Wojnarowicz uses throughout his writings to be continuously engaging and charming. He's never rude or vulgar, never condescending or occult, always sensitive and struggling to be as honest as written language will permit. Does mist whip at faces? Well, it does something slightly violent to cold faces on a ferryboat. And the syntax of "...talking to my friend next to me whom I met at the airport": only a person with a fresh, anxious relation to the importance of grammar could write this. That *whom* is heartbreaking; it reminds me of my younger self, of the difficulty I have had with the rules of language that promised either to enable or prevent an adequate means of expression. Even now, I make grammatical mistakes, and in my twenties I was often humbled by a grammarian boss who corrected my use of words such as *hopefully,* a word I misused all the time. The same boss also once pointed out to me that I had just used the word "at" unnecessarily, thus recalling for me a whole culture back in Ohio, where I grew up, that often shunned the subtleties of communication. But the rules about *who* and *whom* are confusing even to editors and cunning linguists, and my hat is off to young David for that wonderful *whom*, whether it's correct or not (and I believe it is). As the journal-writer gets older, his grammar, in fact, gets looser and less concerned with being correct, more concerned with being expressive. Wojnarowicz had, to say the least, a vigorous relation with the language, and his journal entries are all fascinating and many of them are deeply moving.

Take for example another entry made about twenty days into the Outward Bound journey. David has been dropped onto lonely Babbitch Island, where he is expected to spend several days alone, surviving without having brought along food or equipment. On his second day, his spirits are still good; he swims and finds some edible plants; he takes a nap.

I just woke up and feel a bit better. I am not so hungry so I will fast until tomorrow. Then that will mean one more day and I will be back again. It is very strange when you don't use your voice for a period of time. You begin to realize how quiet things are and how beautiful nature is. I hear all kinds of birdcalls while I am writing this. At times I try to answer the call but some are too beautiful which makes it difficult.

The First Time I Met Frank O'Hara

In all of Thoreau there is nothing much lovelier than this, from a teenager who had already worked the streets of Times Square. I was a hustler for a while, too, and I feel a connection to Wojnarowicz, though I had the advantage of being older and thereby, perhaps, a little less vulnerable and impressionable. It's as if there are, in my mind, several lines connecting us; I'm drawn to Wojnarowicz not just by his writing, but also by his personal history, which is somewhat like my own, and by his fragility and his capacity for being amazed. I feel as if we should have been friends, if only we'd met when we were both moving around New York City in the late '80s and early '90s. Wojnarowicz's death represents, for me, the end of a century that felt entirely different from the one we've begun to live in now. If it could be said that the Gay Century started with, say, Wilde's 1891 essays or his 1894 "Phrases and Philosophies," one could also say that the century ended in 1992 or thereabouts when AIDS killed Wojnarowicz and so many others.

‹◊›

Known also for his work in painting, photography, and AIDS activism, Wojnarowicz's name will probably endure longest as the author of a few unforgettable books, most of which are autobiographical and in the form of journals and memoirs. His account, in the diaries, of becoming ill and approaching death from complications resulting from AIDS is among the most unsentimental, concise, and devastating chronicles of our time. Though his death at the age of thirty-seven on July 22, 1992, was one among many such deaths in the early '90s, his came to symbolize for me the loss of a type of gay urban artist that seems a phenomenon of the past—the young man who turns his intense experience with sex, drugs, and people into a unique blend of photography, drawing, painting, and writing. An artist like Wojnarowicz didn't make decisions about his work so much as he deftly found the appropriate place in his work for the various elements of his world. The education of such an artist was provided by life itself, for a high price; he picked up books from lovers, learned how to take photographs from friends; he wrote so well because he had nothing to lose. His brutal honesty cut through everything. As he himself wrote in 1981, Wojnarowicz's work deals with "quiet desperation rather than universal beauty," and the effect he hopes for is for people to "reel from contact with it," to "faint at the meaning" of it. Approaching the end of the diaries and his horrifyingly quick and premature demise, the reader nearly does faint, not so much at the meaning of it as from the lack of meaning, the unacceptable, blunt barricade that suddenly comes up between him and life.

There's an eerie premonition of what's to come in an undated entry sometime during the year 1981. David's friend Peter Hujar is photographing Ethyl Eichelberger in Hujar's East Village apartment (which Wojnarowicz took over after Hujar's death and is where Wojnarowicz died). Hujar was the most talented photographer of his generation, and Eichelberger is said to have been a theatrical genius in drag.

> I got him on the phone from the street below, explained I had the book with me: Hi, Peter. I saw some flashes of light coming from your window, wanted to know if you're okay. He laughed and said come on up for a second. Upstairs Ethyl was sitting on a chair below some extremely bright floodlamps, huge painted face topped with an enormous wig shaped like a bundle of laundry. I said hello and gave Peter the book and left. At the door I turned to him and said, It's gonna be a great decade. Ethyl shouted: I HEARD THAT!!!

By the end of that decade, the 1980s, Hujar and Eichelberger, both in their fifties, were dead, along with so many others, followed shortly by Wojnarowicz himself.

‹◊›

In 1989, the French philosopher Felix Guattari wrote of Wojnarowicz, "This painter-writer is unique in the sense that he fully subordinates his creative process to the daily disclosures in his life." Nowhere in Wojnarowicz's work are those daily disclosures more urgently made and felt than in that most intimate of forms, his diaries, which he kept sporadically, with long periods of frustrating silence (one would like an entry for every day of this artist's life). In 1977, in his early twenties, he wrote about downtown New York as if it were the most interesting place in the world, and in certain ways it surely was. "At night the whores come out along with pimps and everyone struts in high-heeled regalia under the glitter of a half-dead moon and fluorescent lights and lamp poles. Small kids with their trusty collarless dogs dash through it all." Even his dreams—and there's usually nothing more boring than other people's dreams—are described in such a way that makes them ring with energy and pulsing, psycho-sexual life. "Had a hopelessly beautiful dream—whole landscapes sliding by at a rapid pace, retarded child imagery, lots of body movement, embracing. One old guy reappearing quite often in the frames, married and exuding all kinds of strange sexual energies."

He falls in love, goes to Paris, takes drugs, worries about his work, and suffers his share of anxiety, depression, and nagging doubt. But always he finds a way, when he writes at all, to make his words cut through what he feels to be the stupefying mass of other people's words, pictures, images, and meanings. In 1978, in France, he broods on the subject of insanity and feels close to an intimate understanding of it. Just then, as if some strange deity produced it, Wojnarowicz sees the most bizarre animal, a kind of "bristly piglike" thing "scratching at the earth." It's a grisly sight.

> But somehow it seemed right. After all, here I was in the center of Paris, in the center of life itself, my life, a foreign animal who seemed not to belong anywhere anymore: the irises, retinas, the spherical orbiting balls in this head seeing everything now from a strange and unimaginable distance, like the distances of the forest in the eyes of the fish, in the sea swirling round within the thick blue heart of the horse. I wanted to embrace that hyena, that spotted bristled pig, lay down and pummel the earth alongside it, looking for the door, the door that leads away, the entrance into some semblance of recognizable and believable environment, something soothing for this weary heart, this weary head, something that would enable the two of us, foreign brothers in blood, brains, and sight, to lay back drifting, drifting on a huge and warm vellum of polar ice, in the Ferris wheel of night and do nothing else but stay up and trade blood with the stars, with the showering tails of lonely comets while a fragrant blue veil of life drifts through the night and makes us its own.

This is the heart and soul of gay American writing, from Walt Whitman in the 1850s onward. In it are traces of Whitman's lusty music, Thoreau's lyrical insistence on the adequacy of nature, and Emerson's American philosophy of self-determination and pantheism. It's completely up-to-date, perennially fresh, and older, in spirit, than the United States Wojnarowicz had traveled from and would return to.

The New Century

OF ALL GAY WRITERS, David Wojnarowicz's struggle for freedom was the direst struggle of all—he was fighting for his life, and he lost it. Before him, gay writers could afford to toy with the language, to tease out the meaning they were onto while at the same time protecting themselves against being judged unacceptably immoral, decadent, or vulgar. By the time Wojnarowicz had begun his work as a writer, there was a concurrent struggle, which ended in victory (and which Wojnarowicz played a role in as an activist with his comrades in ACT UP), for full, permanent, legal and moral acceptance of homosexuality in the Western world. This victory (which was not unqualified—there will always be a more or less powerful, malicious lunatic fringe—but was nonetheless a serious ethical, spiritual, and political victory) was made possible in part by the grim spectacle of people dying everywhere of AIDS. The success of this public relations coup, this large-scale sympathetic persuasion, was the result of tireless, passionate men and women taking every opportunity for more than a decade to force gay people and their plight, both as an endangered group and as an unfairly shunned one, into the consciousness of everyone, everywhere, as often, as dramatically, and as meaningfully as possible. It worked. Much of the world, however reluctantly, took note, and actually changed for the better.

The elephantine mainstream American culture, always a reflection of popular opinion, has accordingly availed itself of images and ideas that represent gay people in an open way that could not have been foreseen in the 1950s. Even in the 1970s, gay liberation was a radical, small-scale political movement, something like the good tree-hugging environmentalists now (and they too, we can hope, will have their day of victory, perhaps when the world runs out of oil). Now American culture not only accepts gays and lesbians; it turns a pretty profit from us. The businesspeople that run our popular culture recognized an opportunity and they seized it, grabbing a big, rich new demographic without losing any of the others. They're only too happy to throw us a gay character here, a lipstick lesbian there; they're delighted, in fact, because everyone, gay, straight, or in between, according to the marketing polls and focus groups, enjoys the glimpses we get now of well-behaved, clean, mostly white, amusing homosexuals on TV. What's not to like?

But gay culture itself—the accompaniment to and product of a great struggle—died out with David Wojnarowicz. What was uniquely gay in the realms of art and expression were all the volatile, high-flung, artificial, defensive, clever, beautiful gestures and inventions that gay people had learned, over the course of the twentieth century, to display as proof of their genius. Gay American writers, from Fitz-Greene Halleck to Jane Bowles and Andrew Holleran, had internalized this defensive stance and thereby produced poems and narratives that had a kind of secret energy, an exciting linguistic pressure that was produced in reaction to the homophobic social pressure not to allow themselves to be too revealing of their sexual feelings. This defensive position helped these writers to produce some of the finest writing in all of the world's imaginative literature.

‹◊›

In the most recent years, gay American writing has necessarily changed in drastic ways—there is no longer any political reason for writing in "code." Being openly gay does no damage to an American writer's reputation now—Gore Vidal is surely among our most successful writers and he has been open about his homosexuality—however strange his version of it may be—since at least 1948. Many of our most widely read and admired living authors are openly gay: Michael Cunningham, Dorothy Allison, David Leavitt, Blanche McCrary Boyd, Edmund White, Felice Picano, Fenton Johnson, James McCourt, Rita Mae Brown, Allan Gurganus, Craig Lucas, Mark Matous, Sarah Schulman, Eileen Myles, Terrence McNally, May Sarton, Mark Merlis, and many others. Any "gay novel" written now—even one by an author with a hard-edged, subversive, or intensely homoerotic tone (like Dennis Cooper, for example, or John Rechy)—is situated within the mainstream, and there is every reason to believe that given good enough marketing and enthusiastic "word of mouth," the work will reach a portion of the mainstream book-buying audience and attract some attention from the culture at large rather than exclusively from gay men and lesbians.

We no longer have to address only ourselves; and that happy fact has already changed our work. Homosexuals (in the West) now blend so well, without being in the closet, into the socioeconomic habitat that we have, as a distinct *cultural* force, disappeared. Which is oddly suitable for us, since we have always craved invisibility, for whatever mysterious reason. We've always wanted to be both openly and fully ourselves and, at the same time, to be no more present than a ghost, haunting the page, the stage, the song, the streets. As Wojnarowicz put it toward the end of his short life, "I am disappearing but not fast enough."

There's no longer the danger of (or any danger *in*) being caught in the act of being gay. But there is the possibility that our fearlessness will lead us toward a kind of confusion, a feeling of being lost amid the mainstream crowd that is oblivious not only to our sexual difference from them but, more importantly, oblivious of our difference (and *everyone's* difference) altogether, that is to say, oblivious to individuality. And we, following the lead of the culture we live within, risk losing our own sense of being different in some fundamental and interesting way from the "normal" people; just as a person living among strict conformists (in high school, for instance) can lose sight of the redeeming fact that every person has some difference from all other people and that that represents a fact about the world that is the opposite of trivial. The meaning of life, it seems to me, must be the result, to some extent, of each of us being an individual distinct from every other person. That is, among other things, what the literary products of gay culture can remind us of—that difference is meaningful and valuable in itself; that significance and value are derived more often from surprise encounters and awkward confrontations than from an easy and comfortable relation between habitual collaborators.

Wojnarowicz, toward the end of his very short life, had the voice of confrontation *par excellence:* "Sometimes I come to hate people because they can't see where I am. I've gone empty, completely empty and all they see is the visual form; my arms and legs, my face, my height and posture, the sounds that come from my throat."

That was the voice with which we ended the Gay Century: a voice I'm proud of for its refusal to die quietly and for its power to hold us rapt, even now, in the first decade of a century that is already very different from what I remember of the long-lived 1900s.

‹◊›

Gay people in the twenty-first century will be increasingly assimilated into the world, especially in the United States, where great progress has already been and continues to be made to protect us from homophobia and repression. There will probably always be rednecks and Republicans; but there will always be a few queens and fairies and sissies, too (I hope). As for literature, I believe gay writing will continue to find a large, diverse audience. Great writing has always been a source of more questions than answers; but its universal appeal can also demonstrate to what extent people of all types and persuasions can agree that a given question is worth asking. We are reminded by the best literature of any period or place that the hardest questions, the most mysterious mysteries, are shared by *all* of us, now and forever.

"UNTIL I WAS IN COLLEGE," writes the poet Henri Cole in an essay called "How I Grew," "I had no artistic friends. My only dialogue was with God, whom I besieged with my prayers. For several years, I lived alone in a tree house in the woods behind our suburban Virginia home. It was there that I learned the true meaning of the state-of-being necessary to become a writer, the state of exile and aparthood."

I have, I suppose, a predilection for artists who feel exiled and apart, as most gay writers, and most geniuses, always have. All the writers I've briefly discussed here have, I believe it's fair to say, been haunted to some degree by the feeling that they were in some sense or another in exile and apart not only from the masses of people in the world but even from those to whom they were closest and most intimate. Thoreau, Whitman, Melville, Dickinson—surely they all had some private experience of the feelings of exile and "aparthood." Their work—invariably just words inscribed on paper—silently but unmistakably lays out the evidence of such experience. *Moby-Dick*, perhaps the greatest accomplishment in all of American narrative prose, is surely about nothing if not exile and aparthood; what Ahab and Ishmael and Queequeg and, in a way, even the whale itself, are all suffering from in Melville's seemingly endless story is the never-closed distance between each of them and every other thing, every form of real contact, glory, or redemption. The Whitman of the battlefields cries not only for the sadness of beauty's demise; he suffers also from the feeling he has of being existentially apart from that beauty, with only slight and temporary suggestions along the way of a reliable and comfortable intimacy. The possibility of perennial return to a familiar intimacy is never assured for Whitman; it's never assured for any of us—it's the emotional situation we all seem to want and not to want, to seek and spurn simultaneously. We're all aching for intimacy of the lasting variety; but we seem always to be just growing into it, preparing ourselves for it.

This theme of a just-inaccessible intimacy is given an unforgettable treatment in a six-part poem that closes Henri Cole's magnificent 2003 collection *Middle Earth*. The poem's title, "Blur," gives the simplest possible name to the experience Cole recalls of confusion that seems to be love, of the turbulent mixing of feeling that the erotic sometimes causes when we're drawn to someone, over time, for more than just that one reason—when we really like someone and entertain the thought of holding onto him, and allowing ourselves to be held onto. Cole seems to be thinking, as he starts this meditation on the connection between sex and love, of our tendency to find correlations with ourselves in the past, in the history of our behavior as a species. The story of human beings evolving from whatever we started out as to whatever it is that we've become is, for Cole, the historical background against which his poems are situated. Our relation to the animal kingdom—and our instinctual life within it—is part of the meaning we can take from human life, if we keep aware of it, as the poet does. Cole suffers from an exquisite sensibility; he is too sensitive for his own good; but it allows him access to a unique and powerful poetry.

I.

It was a Christian idea, sacrificing
oneself to attain the object of one's desire.
I was weak and he was like opium to me,
so present and forceful. I believed I saw myself
through him, as if in a bucket being drawn
up a well, cold and brown as tea.
My horse was wet all summer.

I pushed him, he pushed me back—proud, lonely,
disappointed—until I rode him,
or he rode me, in tight embrace, and life went on.
I lay whole nights—listless, sighing, gleaming
like a tendril on a tree—withdrawn
into some desiccated realm of beauty.
The hand desired, but the heart refrained.

‹◊›

"The great works of American literature," according to the great gay American critic Richard Poirier, "are alive with the effort to stabilize certain feelings and attitudes that have, as it were, no place in the world, no place at all except where a writer's style can give them one." I believe there is some truth to the claim that our gay writers have been subject to a particularly intense, urgent struggle to find within themselves a style that would "stabilize" those otherwise homeless "feelings and attitudes"—to bring out from inside them certain considerations that are created and illuminated in part by their sexuality. I wonder if a straight man could arrive at the simile for himself that Henri Cole comes to after "whole nights" of emotional withdrawal and erotic need: "like a tendril on a tree."

It is hardly necessary to acknowledge that most of the best poets, writers, musicians, and painters throughout world history have been heterosexual and have been anything but handicapped or restricted by being in the sexual majority. The writer who was, for me, the greatest in the last decade of the twentieth century, W. G. Sebald, was as far as I know as straight as they come—the German writer lived quietly with his wife and family in England until his tragic death in December 2001.

The First Time I Met Frank O'Hara

Nevertheless, there has been and still is something about gay American writers as a group that has emerged gradually and majestically; the gay sensibility among writers in the United States has evolved beautifully, and it deserves our respect and attention. Though there is no place in the world anymore for a living gay culture, exactly, because there is no need for one, there is still and will always be a sensibility that is affected by, informed by, helped along by aspects of being gay in a world in which most people are not. There has been and will continue to be something special about gay artists—something we can continue to admire and encourage. Being gay enables some people to appreciate the beauty of, and indeed to thrive on, "the state of exile and aparthood." There is, after all, a state of grace—a condition of personal elegance or dignity—that seems to accompany all worthy efforts; and living openly and honestly, whether gay or straight or something in between, is for all of us self-evidently worth doing. The difficulty of doing so—which has been and may still be greater for gay people—only refines the grace. Living in such a way—without deliberate deceit or moral compromise—along with doing one's work, is I believe the "only path of escape known in all the worlds of God," to quote again from the immortal Emerson's book on *The Conduct of Life.* It is the only means whereby we can be released from our spiritual heaviness.

‹◇›

Henri Cole's first collection, *The Marble Queen,* appeared in 1986, and clearly reflected a painstaking history of reading, thinking, and writing leading up to it, fully formed and accomplished as it is. That first collection, like so many books of the last twenty years by gay men, is dedicated to a man who died young: John P. Sawyer

(1952-1985). Cole began his career with *The Marble Queen* as a poet of confident clarity and sense, qualities that still inhere in his new, more complex work. "Of Island Animals," in the first book, ends with: "Tonight my body is a slip of moon, / a leafy glen in autumn / offering its light to you for nothing." Cole has always had a gift for using a language of striking beauty, limpidity, and an almost Japanese sense of things being placed without fussiness but with just the right spirit of care and calm attention (he was born in Japan). Cole is very careful, but not at all safe or effete.

The Visible Man, in 1998, prompted Harold Bloom to say that "Cole will be a central poet of his generation." That book, Cole's fourth, contained one of my favorite of his poems, "The Coastguard Station," which is for me as central a poem of our time as any other. It's a poem about self-consciousness and self-image, the wish to be included and blessed, and a troubling ambivalence about our relations to other people and with ourselves. "At dawn," it begins, "a few recruits have a smoke / on the patio above the breakers; / across the sand path, I sit with my book, / hearing their animal coughs." The mood of the poem is typical of Cole's work generally: pensive, nervous, on the edge of violence, uneasy within a chosen solitude that's almost identical with loneliness. The poem ends: "To myself, womanish, conflicted, subservient, / like Esau pleading, 'Bless me also, Father!' / I hate what I am and I hate what I am not." We've never had a more poignant expression of ambivalence. And what are we, nowadays, if not ambivalent?

‹◊›

Middle Earth, Cole's fifth book, represents the most affecting contemporary linguistic music that I know of. There's a disarming hon-

esty and directness about these poems, and an astonishing feeling of the newborn. The opening lines of the new book give an impression of being totally without anxiety about the past, perfectly alone in the land of words, oblivious and wondrously indifferent to (though not at all ignorant of) their multifarious prior uses. "Born," Cole whispers, "I was born. / Tears represent how much my mother loves me, / shivering and steaming like a horse in rain."

This unassuming gay poet, Henri Cole, who was raised in Virginia, has found a way—by cutting through the unimportant big ideas, by narrowing in on the eternally fascinating complexity of human desire—to pick up for us and examine, for a moment of heightened and sublime introspection, our need for connection to another person, which is, after all, the trait that defines us as social beings intent on being fully ourselves. Here's the last part of "Blur," our finest poem at the start of this frightening new century:

> 6.
> In front of me, you are sleeping. I sleep also.
> Probably you are right that I project
> the ambiguities of my own desires.
> I feel I only know you at the edges.
> Sometimes in the night I jump up panting,
> see my young gray head in the mirror
> and fall back, as humans do, from the cold glass.
> I don't have the time to invest in what
> I purport to desire. But when you open
> your eyes shyly and push me on the shoulder,
> all I am is impulse and longing
> pulled forward by the rope of your arm,
> I, flesh-to-flesh, sating myself
> on blurred odors of the soft black earth.

SINCE HIS RETURN FROM PERU in the 1950s, where he lived with the headhunters he would later write about in his classic memoir *Keep the River on Your Right*, Tobias Schneebaum has traveled to most of the hardest-to-reach and least visited places in the world. But the one place he has returned to over and over again with passion and devotion is Asmat, a swampy section of New Guinea in the southern part of Irian Jaya. Asmat gets two hundred inches of rain each year, an average of one inch for each of the 200 days it rains there. Until recently, the Asmat people, like the natives of Peru Tobias had lived with, were known as violent, headhunting cannibals. It is these people that Tobias goes to extraordinary pains to be among for as long as he can arrange for (the difficult journey from New York to Asmat, involving several planes, boats, and canoes, takes three days). He always comes back to New York, but he's forever going to New Guinea again to live in the mud, where there is nothing much to eat ("no fruit, no beef, hardly ever any vegetables"), where he sleeps on the floor, and where he has somehow been happiest and most fully alive.

I have known Tobias for many years—he is one of my closest friends; and he is among the most open and honest of people. In his new book, *Secret Places: My Life in New York and New Guinea*, he reveals himself in a way, and to an extent, that he had never done before. This is the spiritual memoir of a man now in his eighties who's spent most of his life actively searching for an acceptable, enlivening spirituality. He has thought about and considered (and passed over) many of the world's religions and beliefs; he's Jewish;

he's gay. But he was never quite able to commit himself to an existing system of religious belief until he went to Asmat and lived with people who were connected to each other and to the spirits as they are there. "The bird life, the animal life, the river, the forest and all the plant life, all the human life, the way the Asmat live and work, the way they commune with spirits of the dead through their carvings, the whole manner of their physical lives—all combine," he writes, "to form a way that I wanted to have lived myself."

I've chosen to end with Tobias not because his new book particularly represents the twenty-first century or the future of gay writing; but because he has spent a lifetime as a writer asking the questions that are the most persistent and urgent for all the gay writers I have come to love: Who am I? and How should I live?

‹◊›

The epigraph to *Secret Places,* Tobias's *Pilgrim's Progress* story, is by another seeker and skeptic, William Blake, and the lines work in an eerie way to guide the reader through the book:

> We who dwell on Earth can do nothing of ourselves,
> every thing is conducted by Spirits.

That space between *every* and *thing* gives me a spooky feeling; it puts a strange emphasis on the physical aspect of Blake's idea, which comes from his long poem *Jerusalem.* The space between the words seems to suggest that it's not merely *everything* in a general way that is conducted by Spirits: it's that every single thing in the world—all that we can see and all that we cannot see, ourselves, our computers, our homes, our clothes, our trees and animals, our food—each thing has within it Spirits that control it, determine its fate, its life. Though we all do all sorts of things, and though much of our behavior seems to be willed and chosen and controlled, we also know that we do no thing without the influence of the past working its own spooky magic on us.

The Asmat people spend much of their time taming and befriending the spirits that they believe are everywhere around them and within themselves; that is, so to speak, their daytime spiritual practice. When the Asmat sleep, their spirits leave their bodies and wander around, returning before daybreak. "To step over someone who is sleeping," Tobias writes, "often leads to the death of that person, for that one stride over the body prevents the spirit from returning to its home in the living being." The Asmat try to avoid the wrath of the spirits (which is known to be terrible, sometimes fatal) and they extol the spirits to guide them and to show them the truth. The artwork the Asmat have been making for a long, long time is now represented in major museums around the world, partly due to Tobias's efforts (he is perhaps the world's foremost expert on the subject). Some of the finest Asmat art is in Tobias's apartment in Greenwich Village: war shields, drums, paddles, spears, ancestor figure carvings, daggers for ritual killings, and necklaces of human vertebra, dog teeth, pig teeth, and flying-fox teeth. For Christmas this year, he brought a headhunting armband to decorate our tree. All of the work made by Asmat carvers is believed to contain a spirit; much of the work is made to commemorate a person that died. For Tobias, the best of the Asmat carvings are the older ones, those made by people uninfluenced by the West. The new work, while often impressive, rarely has the spiritual quality about it that is, for Tobias, the significance, the meaning, of the work. He remembers seeing a carver at work long ago. "It is as though the carver and the spirit of the dead man for whom the carving would be named spoke to each other in whispers, softly, in order to tender to each other's needs. Surely, that spirit was close by, perhaps to induce some particularly personal element through which the man's family could recognize him. Contact with one's deceased relatives is only natural. The living want to avenge the dead; the dead want to go on in peace to the Land of the Dead." The practice of headhunting was one means for the Asmat to avenge their dead. Now that headhunting is in the past—the Christian missionaries have intervened—perhaps it follows that the spirits making their way to the Land of the Dead must avenge their own deaths. In any case, nightfall in Asmat seems to bring out "any number of spirits, good and evil."

It's not easy for me to understand why my friend Tobias should want to live in such an inhospitable, scary place. He knows this, and he seems to speak to his friends in this book when he gives a persuasive and touching explanation. "Throughout my life, I have been searching for a way to connect to other human beings and find that among people like the Asmat, who live in a world of spirits, I can lose my insecurities and be content. I watch the men of Asmat and try in some way to emulate them. At night, at times, we huddle and embrace."

‹◊›

In the late 1970s, during one of his long stays in Asmat, Tobias was sitting in a house with four Asmat men who were known to be sorcerers. It was unusual for these men to speak about their practices; but with the passing of cannibalism and headhunting, other things changed as well, and he found these men willing to tell him what they had formerly kept strictly as secrets. They talked about their methods of relieving pain and of drawing enemies toward them.

Tobias told them of a time when he'd been fishing with a chief and his family. They happened upon a group of people and the chief would call out to them, "Come to us, people of Omandesep, so we can kill and eat you. Come to us!" The heads of enemies, in the past, Tobias remarks, "were taken when the opportunity and need arose," but headhunting had probably never been practiced among the Asmat "as frequently and devastatingly as it had been only a few miles to the north. . . ."

That same day, huddled with the four sorcerers, while listening to a story told by one of the Asmat men, Tobias had a hallucination that permanently changed his outlook and his spiritual condition. A man called Tete was telling of the death of his wife in childbirth just a few months earlier. He was very angry about her death—he "wanted to kill all the women who were pregnant" and he made a horn from a *tu* tree which he blew every evening to make the pregnant women die. While many of the women got sick after hearing the horn, none died. "Tete's sorcery had not been powerful enough." But since the Asmat believe that any death not caused by old age is the fault of some other person, and must be avenged, a brutal ceremony was held to find the person responsible for his wife's death.

Her body was wrapped in leaves and placed on a platform, with a bow and long arrows placed on the mat. The women relatives were moaning and wailing alongside the platform as it was carried; they rolled around in the mud "in order to keep the spirits from recognizing them. Recognition would lead the spirit of Tete's wife to try to enter another body and control it." The bone from a cassowary bird was put into a fire, taken out, and pressed onto the dead woman's covered head. Her body was then pointed in the direction of other villages, and Tete asked the spirits if someone from each of the villages in turn had caused his wife's death. His questions to the spirits were filled with lamentation and misery. "Oh, why did you die? Why did you leave me? Tell me who it was who killed you. Was it someone from the village of Pirien?" Nothing happened. He asked the spirits about all of the surrounding villages. Finally Tete asked if someone from his own village had killed her. "There was a pause," Tobias writes, having put himself there in the village, which he knew well, while listening to the story, "somewhere in the atmosphere itself. The universe seemed to stop all movement, as though it were taking a breath." The bow and arrows on the platform "began to shake and make terrible noises." It was a sign from the spirits that someone from Tete's own village had caused the woman's death. Tete immediately began pointing the body in the direction of specific houses in the village, asking if the killer lived there. Finally he pointed the body in the direction of his own house, and the arrows "flashed and flew around in a whirlwind on top of the mat in which the body of Tete's wife was wrapped." He pointed the cassowary bone, which was still on his dead wife's forehead, at his father, his brothers-in-law, and then toward a relative from another village who had been staying with Tete's family. Suddenly "the bone went into the body, and then into the forehead of Tete's wife." Chaos ensued. "At first it seemed that the arrows were murmuring to one another. They suddenly stood on end. They flew into the air, fought with one another, and knocked one another off the platform." Tobias was "completely caught up in the spell of the story," he says, and found himself "side by side with the relative of Tete, watching the body as it was turned slowly, inch by inch, until it was pointing at me. It was my most terrifying moment, changing my concept of the world and of the universe."

The First Time I Met Frank O'Hara

When I read this, I rang up Tobias and asked him if it was to be taken seriously. Or was it meant as a kind of fairy tale? He told me that he believes it was a hallucination, but one shared by the entire village. "It's magic," he said, "and I believe in magic."

‹◊›

Writing about the long process the missionaries in Asmat faced in converting the people there from headhunting and violence to a kind of Christianity, Tobias is modest about a subject he must feel deeply ambivalent about. The Asmat were ready, he says, to give up the warfare and the cannibalism. "It ended easily, quickly.... Christ had taken on the burden of vengeance." Tobias in New Guinea was always concerned more about the people and their real spiritual condition than with taking sides or arguing. In all the years I've known him, I've never known Tobias to argue about anything. "I had no answers then for anyone looking for the way to freedom, the escape route from the real world of spirits. I have no answers now that are not my own secrets. On occasion, I know the relevant questions, but, more often than not, there are no answers."

BIBLIOGRAPHY

Acocella, Joan. *Willa Cather and the Politics of Criticism*. Lincoln: Univ. of Nebraska Press, 2000.

Ashbery, John. *April Galleons: Poems*. NY: Viking, 1987.

Austen, Roger. *Playing the Game: The Homosexual Novel in America*. Indianapolis/NY: The Bobbs-Merrill Company, 1977.

Baldwin, James. *Collected Essays*. NY: Library of America, 1998.

———. *Giovanni's Room*. NY: Dell, 1956.

Berkson, Bill and Joe LeSueur, eds. *Homage to Frank O'Hara*. Bolinas, CA: Big Sky, 1988.

Bernard, Emily, ed. *Remember Me to Harlem: The Letters of Langston Hughes and Carl Van Vechten 1925–1964*. NY: Knopf, 2001.

Boswell, John. *Christianity, Social Tolerance, and Homosexuality: Gay People in Western Europe from the Beginning of the Christian Era to the Fourteenth Century*. Chicago: Univ. of Chicago Press, 1981.

Bowles, Jane. *My Sister's Hand in Mine: The Collected Works*. NY: FSG, 1966/1995.

Campbell, James. *Talking at the Gates: A Life of James Baldwin*. Berkeley, LA, London: Univ. of California Press, 2002.

Canning, Richard. *Gay Fiction Speaks: Conversations with Gay Novelists*. NY: Columbia UP, 2000.

Capote, Truman. *Breakfast at Tiffany's*. 1958. Reprint, NY: Vintage, 1993.

Cavell, Stanley. *The Senses of Walden*. Expanded ed. Chicago and London: Univ. of Chicago Press, 1981.

Chauncey, George. *Gay New York: Gender, Urban Culture, and the Making of the Gay Male World, 1890–1940*. NY: Basic Books, 1994.

Cole, Henri. "How I Grew," The Borzoi Reader online: www.randomhouse.com/knopf/authors/cole/poetsonpoetry.html

———. *The Marble Queen*. NY: Atheneum, 1986.

———. *Middle Earth: Poems*. NY: FSG, 2003.

Crain, Caleb. *American Sympathy: Men, Friendship, and Literature in the New Nation.* New Haven and London: Yale Univ. Press, 2001.

Crane, Hart. *Collected Poems.* 2d ed. Edited by Marc Simon. NY and London: Liveright, 2000.

———. *O My Land, My Friends: The Selected Letters.* Edited by Langdon Hammer and Brom Weber. NY: Four Walls Eight Windows, 1997.

Crase, Douglas. *Amerifil.txt: A Commonplace Book.* Ann Arbor: Univ. of Michigan Press, 1996.

———. "A Voice Like the Day," in *Poetry,* January 1994, pp. 225-238.

De Rougemont, Denis. *Love in the Western World.* Princeton, NJ: Princeton UP, 1983.

Dickinson, Emily. *Open Me Carefully: Emily Dickinson's Intimate Letters to Susan Huntington Dickinson.* Edited by Ellen Louise Hart and Martha Nell Smith. Ashfield, MA: Paris Press, 1998.

Dillon, Millicent. *A Little Original Sin: The Life and Work of Jane Bowles.* NY: Holt, Rinehart and Winston, 1981.

Durkheim, Emile. *Suicide: A Study in Sociology.* NY: Free Press, 1997.

Emerson, Ralph Waldo. *The Conduct of Life.* New and rev. ed. Boston: Houghton, Mifflin and Co., 1885.

Ewing, Max. *Going Somewhere.* NY: Knopf, 1933.

Farr, Judith. *The Passion of Emily Dickinson.* Cambridge and London: Harvard UP, 1994.

Firbank, Ronald. *Five Novels.* NY: New Directions, 1981.

Fitzgerald, F. Scott. *The Great Gatsby.* NY: Charles Scribner's Sons, 1925.

Fone, Byrne R. S. *A Road to Stonewall: Male Homosexuality and Homophobia in English and American Literature, 1750-1969.* NY: Twayne Publishers, 1995.

Ford, Charles Henri. *Water from a Bucket: A Diary 1948-1957.* NY: Turtle Point Press, 2001.

——— and Parker Tyler. *The Young and Evil.* 1933. Reprint, NY: Masquerade Books, 1996.

Fuller, Henry Blake. *Bertram Cope's Year.* 1919. Reprint, NY: Turtle Point Press, 1998.

Genet, Jean. *Querelle.* Translated by Anselm Hollo. NY: Grove, 1974.

Gilman, Richard. *Decadence: The Strange Life of an Epithet.* NY: FSG, 1979.

Goldin, Frederick, trans. and ed. *Lyrics of the Troubadours and Trouveres: An Anthology and a History.* Gloucester, MA: Peter Smith, 1983.

Grobel, Lawrence. *Conversations with Capote.* NY: New American Library, 1985.

Guattari, Felix. "David Wojnarowicz," in *Rethinking Marxism,* Vol. 3 #1, Spring 1990, pp. 76–77.

Halleck, Fitz-Greene. *The Poetical Writings of Fitz-Greene Halleck with Extracts from Those of Joseph Rodman Drake.* Edited by James Grant Wilson. NY: D. Appleton and Co., 1869.

Hallock, John W. M. *The American Byron: Homosexuality and the Fall of Fitz-Greene Halleck.* Madison: Univ. of Wisconsin Press, 2000.

Hardwick, Elizabeth. *American Fictions.* NY: Modern Library, 1999.

———. *Herman Melville.* NY: Viking, 2000.

Harris, Daniel. *The Rise and Fall of Gay Culture.* NY: Hyperion, 1997.

Holleran, Andrew. *Dancer from the Dance.* NY: William Morrow and Co., Inc., 1978.

Huysmans, J. K. *Against the Grain (A Rebours).* NY: Dover, 1969.

Kaiser, Charles. *The Gay Metropolis: 1940–1996.* NY/Boston: Houghton Mifflin, 1997.

Katz, Jonathan Ned. *Love Stories: Sex Between Men before Homosexuality.* Chicago and London: Univ. of Chicago Press, 2001.

Kiernan, Robert F. *Frivolity Unbound: Six Masters of the Camp Novel.* NY: Continuum, 1990.

Kramer, Larry. *Faggots.* NY: Random House, 1978.

Lehman, David. *The Last Avant-Garde: The Making of the New York School of Poets.* NY: Anchor Books, 1999.

LeSueur, Joe. *Digressions on Some Poems by Frank O'Hara: A Memoir.* NY: FSG, 2003.

Lowenfels, Walter. *Walt Whitman's Civil War.* NY: Da Capo, 1960.

Mariani, Paul L. *The Broken Tower: A Life of Hart Crane.* NY: Norton, 1999.

Martin, Robert K. *The Homosexual Tradition in American Poetry.* Austin and London: Univ. of Texas Press, 1979.

Mayer, Bernadette. *Midwinter's Day.* NY: Turtle Island, 1982.

Melville, Herman. *Moby-Dick or, The Whale.* 1815. Reprint, NY: E. P. Dutton, 1950.

———. *Redburn: His First Voyage, Being the Sailor-boy Confessions and Reminiscences of the Son-of-a-Gentleman, in the Merchant Service.* 1894. Reprint, Evanston and Chicago: Northwestern Univ. Press and the Newberry Library, 1969.

Miller, Edwin Haviland. *Melville.* NY: Persea, 1975.

Morris, Roy, Jr. *The Better Angel: Walt Whitman in the Civil War.* Oxford and NY: Oxford UP, 2000.

O'Hara, Frank. *The Collected Poems.* Edited by Donald Allen. NY: Knopf, 1979.

Oke, Richard. *Frolic Wind.* London: Gollancz, 1929.

Phillips, Adam. *Equals.* NY: Basic Books, 2002.

Plimpton, George. *Truman Capote: In Which Various Friends, Enemies, Acquaintences and Detractors Recall His Turbulent Career.* NY: Doubleday, 1997.

Poirier, Richard. *Poetry and Pragmatism.* Cambridge: Harvard UP, 1992.

———. *Trying It Out in America: Literary and Other Performances.* NY: FSG, 1999.

Rosco, Jerry. *Glenway Wescott Personally: A Biography.* Madison: Univ. of Wisconsin Press, 2002.

Rizza, Gerard. *Regard for Junction.* London: Spectacular Diseases, 1992.

Schneebaum, Tobias. *Asmat Images.* Asmat, New Guinea: Asmat Museum of Culture and Progress, 1985.

———. *Keep the River on Your Right.* NY: Grove, 1969.

———. *Secret Places: My Life in New York and New Guinea.* Madison: Univ. of Wisconsin Press, 2000.

Schuyler, James. *Selected Poems.* NY: FSG, 1988.

Scully, Robert. *The Scarlet Pansy.* NY: William Faro, 1933.

Sontag, Susan. *Where the Stress Falls.* NY: FSG, 2001.

Stein, Gertrude. *The Autobiography of Alice B. Toklas.* 1933. Reprint, NY: Vintage, 1990.

———. *Geography and Plays.* 1922. Reprint, Madison: Univ. of Wisconsin Press, 1993.

———. *Lucy Church Amiably.* 1930. Reprint, Normal, IL: Dalkey Archive Press, 2000.

———. *Selected Writings.* Edited by F. W. Dupee. NY: Vintage, 1990.

———. *Wars I Have Seen.* NY: Random House, 1945.

Tate, Allen. *Essays of Four Decades.* 3rd ed. Wilmington, DE: ISI, 1999.

Thoreau, Henry David. *Walden or, Life in the Woods.* 1854. Reprint, NY: Everyman's Library, 1910.

———. *Selected Journals.* Edited by Carl Bode. NY: New American Library, 1967.

———. *A Week on the Concord and Merrimack Rivers.* 1849. Reprint, NY: Penguin, 1998.

———. *Wild Fruits: Thoreau's Rediscovered Last Manuscript.* Edited by Bradley P. Dean. NY: Norton, 2000.

Topsfield, L. T. *Troubadours and Love.* Cambridge: Cambridge Univ. Press, 1975.

Van Vechten, Carl. *The Blind Bow-Boy.* NY: Knopf, 1923.

———. *Excavations: A Book of Advocacies.* NY: Knopf, 1926.

———. *Parties.* NY: Knopf, 1930.

Vidal, Gore. *The City and the Pillar.* NY: E. P. Dutton and Co., 1948.

———. *The City and the Pillar.* Rev. ed. NY: E. P. Dutton and Co., 1965.

———. *Palimpsest: A Memoir.* NY: Penguin, 1995.

Warner, Michael. "Thoreau's Bottom," in *Raritan,* XI:3 Winter 1992, pp. 53–79.

Wescott, Glenway. *Continual Lessons: Journals 1937–1955.* Edited by Robert Phelps with Jerry Rosco. NY: FSG, 1990.

———. *The Pilgrim Hawk: A Love Story.* 1940, Reprint, NY: NY Review of Books, 2001.

Whitman, Walt. *Poetry and Prose.* NY: Library of America, 1982.

Wilde, Oscar. *The Artist as Critic: Critical Writings.* Edited by Richard Ellmann. Chicago: Univ. of Chicago Press, 1982.

Wilson, Edmund. *The Shores of Light: A Literary Chronicle of the Twenties and Thirties.* NY: FSG, 1952.

Wineapple, Brenda. *Sister Brother: Gertrude and Leo Stein.* Baltimore: Johns Hopkins UP, 1997.

Wojnarowicz, David. *Close to the Knives: A Memoir of Disintegration.* NY: Vintage, 1991.

———. *In the Shadow of the American Dream: The Diaries of David Wojnarowicz.* Edited and with an introduction by Amy Scholder. NY: Grove, 1999.

WITH THANKS PARTICULARLY TO
PROFESSOR DAVID FREEDBERG AND MY COLLEAGUES AT
THE ITALIAN ACADEMY FOR ADVANCED STUDIES
IN AMERICA AT COLUMBIA UNIVERSITY

&

MALAGA BALDI;

KATHRYN BELDEN, JOHN OAKES
AND EVERYONE ELSE AT FOUR WALLS EIGHT WINDOWS;
TONI-MARIE ANGELI, TOM DONAGHY, DENNIS DRABELLE,
ANDREW JACOBS, EDITH KELLY, JOHN W. KRAKAUER, MD,
TIM LOVEJOY, DREW MOSLEY, ALEXANDER MYLES, DRU ORENSTEIN,
PAUL SANASARDO, TOBIAS SCHNEEBAUM, DIANE WILLIAMS,
C. HOLMES WOLFE, JR.
JOHN KRENEK AND JAMIE NIBLOCK
RAYMOND HAN AND PAUL KELLOGG

AND MY FAMILY